TABLE OF CONTENTS

Part One—Unveiling the Kingdom Culture

1. In the Beginning 7
2. What is a Kingdom Culture? 13
3. Birthing of the Book 21
4. Build Relationships First 29
5. Diversity and the Power of the Team............................... 33
6. Metron—An Incredibly Vital Scriptural Concept 39
7. How to Discover Your Metron—and Other's 49
8. My Metron Tunnel—Your Metron Tunnel 57
9. The Amazing Pie or Teamwork in Glory! 67
10. Practical Wisdom for the Team... 75
11. Attitudes and Actions That Kill the Culture 87
12. Ownership vs. Territorial—Becoming Familiar with the Difference 95
13. How Does Primary Leadership Fit Into a Team Culture? 103
14. Strong Character—Ingredients for Excellence in the Culture.....113
15. Research Proves the Good Guy *Doesn't* Finish Last...................117

Part Two—Four Absolute Principles of Management

16. The First D—Definition.. 127
17. The Second D—Delegation.. 133
18. The First C—Communication 139
19. The Second C—Confrontation 147
20. Essential Keys to Confrontation 157

21 Indirect Management—The Toxic Alternative to Healthy Confrontation 161

Part Three—Infusing Life into Your Culture

22 The God-Mirror 171
23 Calling to Life 177
24 Heart 185
25 The Virtue of Listening 193
26 Three Vital Habits That Give Life to a Kingdom Culture 205
27 Transition in a Kingdom Culture 211
28 In the Beginning 217

KINGDOM CULTURE

Uncovering the Heart of
What Empowers Teams

BRUCE LENGEMAN

Copyright © 2017 by Bruce Lengeman

All rights reserved. No part of this book may be used, reproduced, stored in a retrieval system, or transmitted in any form whatsoever — including electronic, photocopy, recording — without prior written permission from the author, except in the case of brief quotations embodied in critical articles or reviews.

Scripture quotations marked NKJV , unless otherwise noted, are taken from the *New King James Version*. Copyright © 1982 by Thomas Nelson, Inc. Used by permission. All rights reserved.

Additional Scripture quotations marked YLT are taken from the *Young's Literal Translation*. Public domain.

FIRST EDITION

ISBN: 978-1-946466-15-0

Library of Congress Control Number: 2017940770

Published by

partner publishing

P.O. Box 2839, Apopka, FL 32704

Printed in the United States of America

Disclaimer: The views and opinions expressed in this book are solely those of the author and other contributors. These views and opinions do not necessarily represent those of Certa Publishing. Please note that Certa Publishing's publishing style capitalizes certain pronouns in Scripture that refer to the Father, Son, and Holy Spirit, and may differ from some publishers' styles.

Part One

UNVEILING THE KINGDOM CULTURE

The book you are reading is designed for those who both love people and need them. It is about teams at work, church, in community, marriage, and family—or wherever someone labors with another—*from two people to countless*. It is about valuing others and calling to life the fullness of power in the person beside you. It is also about leading, as much as teaming. Teaming is NOT meant to diminish the power of leading but to compliment it, to empower it, to enhance it, and to, actually, create it. The book you are reading is really about love and the life that exudes from love. The vision for this book is not to give you mere tools to enhance your cause…

…but to *change your life*.

1

IN THE BEGINNING

I usually don't include an "Introduction" in the books I write. That's because some people skip introductions and miss all the essential information it contains. This first chapter is a *vital* introduction for this book you have begun reading.

In deciding to read this book, you have decided to begin a journey—into life, into teamwork, and into leadership. This book is a collection of things I have learned—which God taught me—throughout my four decades of leading in many diverse environments and types of organizations.

What I Expect, What I Predict

I expect and may even go as far as saying, I *predict* that for every hour you spend reading and discussing the principles and ideas in this book, you will save countless hours of putting out crisis fires, resolving interpersonal issues, re-fixing what you thought you had already fixed, or fighting low morale. It will not only save you time, but it will save you heartbreak and confusion. Why waste your energy?

Honestly, the principles in this book may take your team, organization, or even your marriage, from the threat of annihilation—to something awesome and productive.

Most organizations or teams that are struggling, are doing so because they've fail to prioritize foundational principles, many of which I target in this book. So as I write to you, I am hopeful that I will preserve you from needless failures and help you become highly productive in your mission, more than you ever thought possible.

What Should Be in This Book

Every chapter in this book could qualify as a complete book in itself—probably a thick one. The possibilities of topics that could be included are endless. As you read this, you may think of minor exceptions to the principles I promote, applications I have not thought of, or concepts I *should* have included. This is okay and expected. It is not bad. Had I incorporated all that *could* have been included, you would likely not have the strength to lift this book to your lap. Keep this in mind as you read—the real depth and application of this book will come as you and your team—from your spouse, to all the employees in your business, whatever the word *team* means to you—*together* process the concepts you are about to learn. I have also added questions to the end of each chapter to help your team process this information. Go through the discussion question at the end of the chapters and form a *shared vision* for how this book will apply to you and your team.

Though the principles you are about to read apply to both leaders and non-leaders, much of my focus in this book is directed toward leaders. I believe these principles could radically change the way leaders lead and provide the tools needed to achieve greater levels of influence within their spectrum of authority.

The Three Parts to This Book

I often get through three-quarters of many books I choose to read, only to realize that the authors are simply reprocessing the same information from the beginning of the book. At that point, I place the book back on the shelf. I have been careful to ensure that I don't waste your time in the same way as you read this book. Therefore, the last chapters are as vital as the first ones. I divided this book into three different parts, and much like a puzzle—each part is vital. Much of what is in the final part is actually the heart of what is shared in the first two parts.

The first part is *unveiling* the Kingdom Culture, including the definitions and dynamics of what creates a God-honoring culture. The second part is *Four Absolute Principles of Management.* This part addresses core principles for success, which many struggling organizations neglect. The third part is *Infusing Life into Your Culture.* This part is about creating and maintaining a *life-giving spirit* in your culture—the grace, the glory, and the beauty.

Healing from This Book

While sitting over pancakes in a recent meeting with a friend, he let me in on the new things in his life's journey. He told me a horror story of how, a few years ago, he and his wife were victims in an abusive culture. I don't know both sides, and I am not equipped to take sides. Although, I *do* know this man is respected in his present place and quite appreciated. I know he has a heart of gold.

After leaving my friend, it dawned on me that a big purpose for *Kingdom Culture* is to bring about healing. This *healing* may come in different ways. One way, and likely the most desired way, is that people who read this book will realize how, while doing their best in relating to others, they didn't do it well. In realizing this, my hope is that they will seek to restore relationships with those they've adversely affected.

Many of you will process these truths with an organization in mind—business, ministry, church, etc. But I challenge you to apply these concepts to all your personal relationships as well (e.g. your marriage, your children, your friends).

I really do hope that you will send me an email and let me know how this book and workbook have helped to change your culture.

Are you ready for the journey? *Then let's go!*

IN THE BEGINNING
Questions

1. Have you been a victim of emotional abuse or mistreatment in a team or organization? What did you learn from the experience that changed the way you lead others?

2. Have you been healed from that experience?

3. Have you had the privilege of being a part of a healthy and life-giving team? If so, what principles were prioritized within this team?

2

WHAT IS A KINGDOM CULTURE?

Kingdom Culture is the term applied to an environment submitted to the principles of the Kingdom of God. The gospel of the kingdom was the primary focus of the teachings of Jesus. "Jesus came to Galilee, preaching the gospel of the kingdom of God, and saying, 'The time is fulfilled, and the kingdom of God is at hand'" (Mark 1:14-15). In Luke 4:43, He said, "I must preach the kingdom of God to the other cities also, because for this purpose I have been sent." In this book the principles of the kingdom of God are applied to the cultures of organizations, teams, and relationships.

What is a Culture?

Culture is simply *the way of life for a specific group of people.* More specifically, it is *a set of beliefs, practices, values, priorities, or traditions that define how people interact and communicate with each other.* Every business, church, ministry, marriage, or team, has a unique culture—or "personality." And, although all cultures may differ, certain foundational values and principles are common to every healthy culture, enabling them to be exciting and productive—and this is what this book is about.

Too often, division among people occurs because people fail to understand the culture of the environment they are working in. A couple of examples: Historically, American missionaries have been indicted for going to other nations, with a totally different culture, and attempting to "colonize" them by imposing an American value system upon them. Any mature missionary knows that, in order to be effective, they have to labor within the cultural paradigms of the country they are in—even while they are laboring to change aspects of that culture. I live in Lancaster County, Pennsylvania. The culture here is distinctly different than where I grew up in Cumberland County. I do things here that I wouldn't do there, and I won't do things here, that I would do there—because of the personalities of the two cultures.

In "churchianity," people switch churches and expect a certain culture to be present. At times, these people end up causing division in the church because of their disappointment. A culture within a church may be intellectual, spooky, passionate, passive, contemplative, informal, formal, dead or alive.

Secular or Christian Environment?

I also know that many of you reading this are working in secular cultures, as opposed to a faith-based culture. Though I write this book from a Christian perspective, *the principles of the kingdom culture transcend cultures*. I could list a multitude of secular management books that endorse the same principles, yet what I am sharing with you comes from a Christian perspective. These principles work no matter where you are. Although the implementation of these principles may vary from culture to culture, without question, the *real* power in a kingdom culture comes from Christ and His commands.

Zoë: Where Heaven's Culture Is Shared

Regardless of the context of the relationship you are in, my goal with this book is that you would know how to generate life in all of your relationships. The word *life* comes from the Greek word, Zoë (zo-ee), which is translated *life* in the Bible. According to Vine's Expository Dictionary, it means *life as God has it.* Zoë means *life with a quality of satisfaction that yields absolute fulfillment.* Zoë has a divine flair to it. It is more than just happiness. It includes peace, joy, and love. Zoë does not mean living without hardship. Zoë is, ultimately, the bottom line of what *everyone* is searching for. Zoë, though, is not self-centered. True zoë enables one to be *UN*-selfish! *Create a life-giving culture, and people will want to be a part of it!*

It is within a heavenly culture that heaven's zoë is experienced.

What is a Kingdom Culture?

We've defined *culture,* but what is a *kingdom culture?*

Six-Point Definition

A kingdom culture is an environment where
- People are valued
- Diversity is celebrated
- Problems are respectfully solved
- True authority is given deference
- People prefer others above themselves
- Wholesome productivity is maximized

Kingdom culture defines how relationships and organizations succeed. It is an environment conducive to *calling people up higher*, instead of relating to them where they are at the present time.

Sub-Cultures

Kingdom culture is a broad term. Under this general term are many characteristics that reveal unique aspects, or sub-cultures, within the culture. Here are just a few other names that are aspects of

a kingdom culture:
- A culture of...
  - Loyalty
  - Servanthood
  - Generosity
  - Excellence
  - Communication
  - Joy
  - Encouragement
  - Learning
  - Gratitude
  - Productivity
  - Power
  - Honor

Culture of honor is a term often used synonymously with kingdom culture. One of the best definitions of a culture of honor I've ever heard is: "A relational environment where others are celebrated for who they are, without stumbling over who they are not." I do not know who to credit for this quote, but it is a brilliant description of an important aspect of a kingdom culture. These are all aspects of a kingdom culture.

Terminology Empowers People

Every culture has its own lingo. Lingo is significant to the development of any culture. Terminology empowers people to use the concepts learned. Within our leadership group at church, simply the use of the term "kingdom culture" provides a description of who we are as a team. Begin using it in your conversations, and watch how people pick up on the concept. For example, "A more excellent way" is lingo that will be better received than saying, "You did it wrong." In our church, one will commonly hear terms (which I will define throughout this book) such as, *calling to life, God-mirror, crossing pain lines, metron, God-excellence, ownership, territorial,* and many more. As you develop the personality of your kingdom culture, simultaneously embrace a *defining lingo* that becomes a part of who you are and keeps your core values always on the table. Let me say it again, *terminology empowers people to use the concepts learned.*

A Mercy-Based Lifestyle Undergirding the Kingdom Culture

I live in an area of diverse religious groups/churches that embrace law over spirit, despite the amazing passages in the Bible proclaiming freedom from a legal mindset. Life, some believe, revolves around behavior control rather than living from the Spirit and the heart. In so doing, those of this mindset reduce many of the teachings of Jesus into a law or a rule, even though, Jesus was actually teaching about principles of the heart. I want to address one such teaching of Jesus, because it is the foundation stone for kingdom culture.

In the Sermon on the Mount, Jesus taught what *true* freedom looks like, and how to be "complete," as the heavenly Father is complete. In Matthew 5:38-48 and Luke 6:27-36, Jesus taught us to do several things, among them: *Whenever we're struck on one cheek, turn the other cheek, when compelled to go one mile, go two, love our enemies, pray for those who persecute us, bless those who curse us, and pray for those who despitefully use us, lend to those who may not pay us back.*

How Does It Fit with the Culture?

No principle from the Bible has been more important to the success of my marriage with Ruthie than these commands to "overcome evil with good" (Romans 12:21). And, I believe, likewise, that no principle will be more important than this one for your team. Learning to honor this concept in a team is both a journey and a goal. But living it will perpetuate grace within your team.

As a team, whatever your team looks like, endeavor to "esteem others more important than yourself" (Philippians 2:3), to "hide a multitude of sins" (1 Peter 4:8), to go the extra mile, overcome evil with good, to extend mercy to offenses, to value relationship over rightness, and to humble yourself when pride shows it's ugly face.

"If you really fulfill the royal law according to the Scripture, 'You shall love your neighbor as yourself,' you do well" (James 2:8).

The Key to the Kingdom Culture: *Value*

Reverberating throughout this book, will be the theme of *valuing others*—it is what the culture is primarily about. The journey in the culture is learning how to be that vessel who brings others value. In my counseling, I hear story after story from people who have been wounded by organizations, businesses, ministries, or other entities. I have mediated many conflicts. Of course, not everyone who tells me their woes is blameless. Almost always, however, for those who have a legitimate claim to having been violated, being de-valued is at the root of their wound.

It is helpful to remember something, which I will address later in more detail: Valuing others does *not* oppose valuing the vision for the team—actually, they complement each other. Our church leadership team is just finishing a leadership internship, where prospective leaders join our team for a year. At our leadership retreat, each intern was asked to share both the negatives and positives relating to his or her experience over the past year. At the top of the list of what they shared was: "We felt valued, needed, and we were given a voice." They couldn't have said anything more encouraging! We had several flaws in the internship program, but through it all, they all emerged feeling *valued*. Every one of them chose to officially move onto our leadership team.

WHAT IS THE KINGDOM CULTURE?
Questions

1. What adjectives would you use to describe the culture of your team or organization?

2. What does the term "life-giving culture" mean to you?

3. Re-read the six-point definition of a kingdom culture in this chapter. How does each point apply to your team?

4. Discuss the value of this definition of *culture of honor:* A relational environment where others are celebrated for who they are, without stumbling over who they are not.

3

BIRTHING OF THE BOOK

"Thanks a lot!" I said, sarcastically, to Dave on the phone. Dave is a professional worship coach, who also oversees a team of other worship coaches. This particular evening Dave had scheduled a challenging consulting session and wanted me to go along.

"Bruce, I have an appointment with one of my clients, and I was wondering if you would go along with me?"

"Well, Ruthie and I did have some plans for tonight here at home, but nothing imperative—a movie night. When would I have to leave?"

"In five minutes."

Though not excited about missing a movie with my wife, I knew I was supposed to go with Dave. Ruthie gave me a hearty thumbs up, and so I quickly threw on my shoes, gave her a hearty smooch goodbye, and headed out to rendezvous with Dave at the Walmart parking lot.

The purpose of the appointment was to attempt to resolve an escalating collision between the church worship leader, Maxx, and one of the musicians, Jack. Upon arrival, Dave led the meeting, encouraging honest dialogue between the two who were contending. Respectful complaints went back and forth (as did a few *dis*respectful ones).

Dave moderated well. I listened.

As time passed and accusations increased, I became more aware that both of these men had good hearts, but they were in conflict because their culture was out of alignment. At this point, I will not take the space to tell the specifics of the values they had violated, which had caused them to be out of alignment with the a kingdom culture. I will say, though, after all the facts and feelings were submitted, Dave and I presented some of these values to them. Dave and I both departed, sensing that Maxx and Jack had emerged with a fresh understanding of the nature of the tug-of-war between them.

On the way home, Dave asked me if I referred to the kingdom culture principles much in my consulting. I told him, "I think everything I do in my consulting and counseling, whether with churches, businesses, or marriages, is helping people to discover the culture of King Jesus."

As much as believers study the Bible or attend conferences to learn how to live life, the principles of a kingdom culture are, unfortunately, not common knowledge. Divisions between friends, low morale in organizations, marriage/family conflicts, and church splits—could be quenched or healed by operating in a kingdom culture.

Because of this appointment with Dave, a *light bulb* clicked on in my mind, and that night I knew I must write this book!

Living with a kingdom perspective can prevent countless problems and divisions, even within families, and with those who didn't grow up with the blessing of a healthy culture at the heart of family interactions. I am also one of those who did not grow up in such an environment. Because of this, in my early years of parenting and leadership, the principles in this book were not always characteristics of my style. Organically, though, I always had them in my heart. But it was a journey through a learning curve (full of good and bad experiences) that taught me these truths.

No ABC's

Living the culture is not a formula. It is a flowing together of godly behaviors, which is only truly experienced by mature people. Self-centered people poison a healthy culture. On the other hand, a healthy culture is an amazing environment for those same self-centered people to grow, change, and mature—to be called up higher!

Domineering people don't function well within a healthy culture. During the meeting with Dave, Maxx admitted to being high D on the DISC Personality Profile—dominant. We all need D people—they are task and goal oriented. They get things done. That being said, high D's, when not balanced by other profiles, will destroy the culture. They can bulldoze over people to accomplish their agenda—or should I say, they sacrifice people rather than the project. Though Jack had his own set of issues, which flew in the face of the culture, he did feel he was a victim to Maxx's dominance, which he called *control,* and as a result, Jack did not feel valued.

Back to the Meeting

After Dave and I briefly explained to Maxx some of the principles of a healthy culture, he saw his role in a much healthier light. He responded, "I want what you are talking about! I don't want people to feel devalued under my leadership, but I don't know this stuff!"

"You're not supposed to," I said. "You are young. This is a journey. I am still, at sixty, learning how to value people and how to *not* devalue them."

"That's encouraging!" replied Maxx. "I guess I just need more humility."

"No, you don't," I said.

Surprised, Maxx questioned, "I don't?"

"No, Maxx, you need *brutal* humility!

Servant leadership, the way Jesus taught, sometimes takes every ounce of self-denial we can muster up—*extreme humility*. But this kind of humility is not merely a passive rolling over. God made you strong and perceptive for a reason, but now, He wants to show you how your strength can increase your influence.

I could tell that Maxx and Jack were beginning to get it.

Climatizing Before the Journey

My friend, Teresa, just climbed a massive mountain in Nepal, in view of Mt. Everest. The protocol for climbing involved the gradual process of *climatizing,* which means she had to acclimatize, or adjust, her body temperature to the extreme environment she would journey into as she climbed.

As I write this portion of the book, I want to get you acclimated to the journey. Before you start the journey through this book, I want you to know that the grace of the Lord Jesus Christ will be with you. I want you to understand that this book is a pattern, or an ideal. It is a goal, like that of becoming more like Jesus. So please accept the fact that, as we often fail in our attempt to be more like Jesus, from time to time, we will also violate the principles of the culture. No matter how skilled we are at maintaining the culture, we will all meet up with circumstances where we miss it, as we later learn through 20/20 hindsight. Each hard lesson may feel as though it is a step backward, but we can "fall ahead" or "fail forward," and learn from our mistakes. We can, indeed, get better at living the culture. As much as I love Ruthie, and have determined to honor and respect her, things come up where I later realize I had been blind to how my actions hurt her. I then apologize, do better, and move on, knowing Ruthie will say, "We're in this together!"

Knowing that we all "miss it" at times, doesn't lessen the pain. It still hurts when we violate the principles, and it still often hurts others.

For these reasons, I proclaim *grace* over you *and grace* to you, as you begin this journey. For some of you, as you expand your journey into the kingdom culture, you will need grace. For some of you, grace may not be needed for the future but for the past—because as you read what the kingdom culture is designed to be, you may become grieved by ways you have violated it in the past. May you receive God's forgiveness and His grace for anything you need restored. Know that "today is the first day of the rest of your life!"

Working with people is complex. I've been in situations where no matter what decision I made, someone was hurt. Such environments are not uncommon to those in leadership. But we do the best we can by following the guidance of the Holy Spirit, the best we know how, and we walk forward in faith.

So again, on every page, remember, "Grace, Grace!"

The Feel-Good Club—What a Kingdom Culture is Not!

Another aspect of your climatizing process is combating false mindsets, which may attach to some who are recovering from failure. Those who have never lived in a kingdom culture may tend to go to the other extreme and become too careful in order to try and make everyone happy. I challenge you to not overreact after you've failed. Instead, find the perfect *balance* of truth.

What *balance* am I referring to? The kingdom culture is not weak. It has a masculine side and a feminine side. It is steel and velvet at the same time. On one hand, nurturing the emotions of others is vital. On the other hand, *truth cannot bow to emotions.* Everyone can feel needed and significant. But, at the same time, our missions are not just to make people *feel* good. There is something to be accomplished beyond having our feelings soothed. A kingdom culture can be severely misinterpreted as a *feel-good club,* where "feeling good" is the goal for everybody.

God forbid!

The kingdom culture undergirds success—whether you call it fruitfulness, productivity, pro-activity, or any other term. Whether your team is your marriage, an elder team, or your business organization, your mission will be greatly enhanced by mastering the values and principles of a kingdom culture.

I trust you will read the rest of this book with these clarifications in mind.

Now, let's talk about some of foundations that support a kingdom culture.

BIRTHING OF THE BOOK
Questions

1. How can the biblical concepts of esteeming others as more important than yourself (Philippians 2:3), loving with the kind of love that hides a multitude of sins (1 Peter 4:8), and overcoming evil with good (Romans 13:21), be applied in practical ways within a kingdom culture?

2. You desire to effectively execute the principles of a kingdom culture in you organization, but the reality is that, at some point, you will do something *not* in alignment with a kingdom culture. What do you think are some healthy ways to recover from mistakes—mistakes that often hurt others?

3. Are you good at nurturing relationships within your team or organization? How can you improve?

4

BUILD RELATIONSHIPS FIRST

The Amazing Trick Test

I would guess that both you and I have been tricked, at some point in our younger years, by that infamous test of following directions. At the top of the paper (in bold) are the words: **YOU ONLY HAVE FIVE MINUTES TO COMPLETE THIS TEST!** There are twenty-five instructions such as: Draw five squares on the back of this paper; Shout your middle name aloud; Count how many single-digit numbers are on this page, etc.

The important instructions of this test, which you are not told, are *only* in number one, number two, and number twenty-five. Number one says, "Read everything before beginning." Number two says, "Put your name in the upper right-hand corner." Number twenty-five says, "Now that you have finished reading everything carefully, do only instructions one and two!" In our haste to win and get a high score, we ignore the traditional *read everything first* command and we zip along our merry way.

Teams are like this test sometimes—in fact, quite often. Teams are off doing what they are supposed to do, forgetting to heed the main thing. When they get to number twenty-five, unfortunately, they are told to go back to number one, which says: *First: Build relationships with your team!* Everything in this book is based on *number one* being in place. If it is not, go back to number one, and do it.

AXE or ACTS!

It was my first elder's retreat as the new pastor of ACTS Covenant Fellowship. I hardly knew the leadership team I had inherited. I knew my first assignment was to obey *number one,* or I would not be successful as the new pastor of this church. We had some agenda items at that retreat, but they were secondary to all of us learning about each other. I told them, "How can I lead with you if I don't know you? How can we work together if we don't know about each other?"

The value of *number one* was already somewhat in place at ACTS when I got there, but I was assigned to perpetuate it and make it grow. *Number one first* became our culture and it still is. We are not perfect at it, and we're still learning how to do it better, but it is at the foundation of most of what we do.

As a foundation for the kingdom culture, no principle is more important than *relationship building.* I've often quoted Theodore Roosevelt's famous saying: *"Nobody cares how much you know until they know how much you care."* In business, commonly, people will stay at their job long-term if they feel relationally fulfilled, even if they can get better pay elsewhere.

My Customer-Relations Seminar and the Kingdom Culture

To add a bit more insight into healthy relationships within a kingdom culture, let me tell you about my customer-relations seminar. After I did this seminar for a restaurant of about eighty employees, one young server told her employer that the seminar had changed her life. In business, developing customer relations has more to do with *who you are*, rather than *what you do*. A customer-service pro is someone who loves people and knows how to express that love.

In many of our marriage seminars, Ruthie and I teach the same thing to couples that we teach in the customer-relations seminars (plus some romantic behaviors that are not applicable for businesses!). At home, we try to develop the habit of smiling when we connect with each other, lots of hugs, and lots of laughs. The kids usually inquire how our day was. Ruthie and I ask about theirs. When I am away for an afternoon, Ruthie never, ever fails to greet me when I come home with a smile, a kiss and a hug—and I, her. It takes a ton of time to hear all about what just happened in our lives while we weren't with each other, but keeping up with the moment is a high priority to us, therefore, we talk a lot about what went on and what's going on.

Your business or church can develop an encouraging atmosphere, just like we try to do at home. You might want to bypass the *kissing* part, but people can be trained to smile, to encourage, to care about what's going on in other's lives, to have "kosher" fun, and when someone comes back from vacation, say, "Welcome back!"

From business to marriage, and everything in between, always remember number one—build relationships first!

BUILD RELATIONSHIPS FIRST
Questions

1. Evaluate your team's culture. Do you prioritize relationships with your fellow team partners, or are you connected only by tasks or professional agendas?

2. How can the business principles of effective "customer relations" practically apply to your team?

3. If you are processing this book as a team, center in on one of the participants who may be struggling in an area of his/her life. Ask how she/he is doing on a personal note, and then show you care by sharing a word of encouragement or a prayer.

5

DIVERSITY AND THE POWER OF THE TEAM

People are like snowflakes—everyone is different.

Pause and think about this: Universally, one major reason conflict exists is that, as much as we can all admit that people are different, we have not learned how to manage diversity—even in seemingly mature environments. In order to create a kingdom culture, we must tap into the *blessing of diversity*.

The next statement may be the most significant truth in this book:

The kingdom culture teaches us not only how to manage diversity but how to *respect* diversity, then, to *celebrate* diversity, and, ultimately, to mutually *benefit* through diversity!

I won't teach a lengthy Bible lesson here, but I will point out to you that 1 Corinthians 12, Romans 12, and Ephesians 4 are all there to remind us that God made us all unique for a wonderful purpose—to express the fullness of who He is through individuality in one body.

Sadly, however, our differences often create more tension than blessings.

Ruthie and I Are Different

Let me use my marriage as a brief example of some of the principles of the culture, which I will expand on as we progress.

At this point, Ruthie and I have been married over four decades. We are each other's best friend. We crave being together and sharing our hearts with each other. But we do not have a great marriage because we are compatible—we are opposites in many areas. Our success is a result of God taking us through a journey to learn a kingdom culture in our marriage.

Our differences have not been our downfall—they have been our strength. Not without friction, not without work, not without tons of talking, not without that brutal humility—our diversity has been the catalyst, which has activated us to become better individuals. It has made us more proficient at working together as an effective team.

Ruthie has taught me more than any other person on earth, by a long shot! And I have stretched her in a healthy way more than anyone else. So therefore, in marriage, the more diversity, the more opportunity to expand personalities, hearts, and impact upon the world. I believe the same potential is available in any team.

The Raw Truth About Unity:
The Time I Wasn't Paid for Speaking

Before jumping into the next chapter, I'll tell you about an experience I had several years ago.

I admit. Nothing was agreed beforehand about payment. My bad for assuming, but I did assume there was a standard payment for this kind of public speaking. Nevertheless, only twice in my multi-decade speaking career did I not get paid when I likely should have, and this was one time. So I am left to guess if what I shared at the annual convention wasn't exactly what they were expecting and maybe that's why I wasn't paid.

My topic was *unity*. The reason I was assigned this topic was that two civic organizations in one town were merging into one, and the convention was *launching* the newly-birthed organization. Perhaps they were expecting a *feel-good, pat-on-the-back* type of address that day. That's not exactly what I gave them.

I'm not an obnoxious speaker, and I despise extremism in addressing crowds, but knowing what was happening, I couldn't simply present a blah, blah, feel-good speech about the glories of unity.

Unity is glorious, but getting there isn't. Disunity is one of the most common villains of life, and unity is one of the hardest virtues in life to maintain.

I told them this.

I said, "*Unity draws blood.*"

We are all created with unique differences. We view life from different perspectives. Our values vary.

Traditionally, historically, commonly, it was (and is) our differences that divide—or create *DIS*-unity. Yet the glory of unity is in finding the glory in diversity. We are all created with unique differences, because God knew that this is the way we would grow stronger and become better. When we learn to celebrate diversity, instead of resisting it, quenching it, denying it, fighting it, dividing over it, or controlling it, we find *a treasure hidden in a field.*

Perhaps I shocked the convention a bit when I said: "You don't need humility to attain unity." I paused and then finished with a phrase I commonly use, "You need *brutal* humility."

Challenging but Not Negative

Unity is the fruit of strong character, maturity, and godliness. Unity is the way of love. It is the outflow of those willing to embrace Paul's words in 1 Corinthians 13:4: "Love suffers long…bears all things…endures all things." And Paul, again, in Philippians 2:3: "Let nothing be done through strife or vainglory; but in lowliness of mind let each esteem other better than themselves." It is embracing Peter's words in 1 Peter 4:8: "Love covers a multitude of sins."

Yep! Unity draws blood. On any level—can't get it any other way. But honestly, that's not necessarily a negative thing. Attaining unity, though hard, is an incredible blessing. It's through the grace of God, the blood of Jesus, and the power of the Holy Spirit, that unity, at any level, can be actualized. I like what Ruthie says to me often when a challenge shows its ugly face, or when we seem to be on different pages: *"No matter what, we're in this together!"* Now *that's* a platform for unity!

"Let us labor to maintain the unity of the Spirit in the bond of peace" (Ephesians 4:3).

So, now, let's explore some of the foundational concepts that will help you understand the fullness of the kingdom culture.

Diversity and the Power of the Team
Questions

1. Why is diversity valuable to any team, business, ministry, or marriage?

2. What are some of the reasons why diversity can cause more faction than favor for a team?

3. What do you think about this statement: "Unity is glorious, but getting there isn't"?

6

METRON—AN INCREDIBLY VITAL SCRIPTURAL CONCEPT

At our leadership-team meetings we always have cookies. Meetings and cookies go together like peanut butter and jelly, or like fried chicken-livers and onions! My aim in this chapter is to make the word *metron* as common a word in your circle as *cookie!* (Or chicken-livers—whichever fits best!) When you learn how important this concept is you will say and hear regularly:

- That's my metron!
- He's in his metron!
- I know what *your* metron is!
- Wow! When she is in her metron, she is powerful!

Metron is a Greek word in the New Testament, which doesn't have an exact translation in English. And because of this, the concept of *metron* has, unfortunately and detrimentally, not been activated. *Metron,* in the Bible, is translated *measure* and *sphere,* but these words do not completely bring out the fullness of the meaning.

Understanding metrons will help you avoid many problems and divisions.

Understanding metrons is central to understanding the kingdom culture.

Understanding metrons is essential for understanding how God created you and how your design fits with others in the body of Christ—even in your marriage.

If you are on a team, you must learn this! I can't overemphasize the importance of every believer and, especially, every leader's need for understanding metrons.

Four-Part Definition of Metron

One: A metron is a measured-out boundary.

As a believer, have you ever felt as though you have to be good at everything? For example, you have to be a prayer warrior, a witness to the lost, a student of the Word, a picketer at abortion clinics, an avid worshipper, a hospital visitor, and so forth. These are all good things, but, too often, spiritual environments perpetuate *cloning,* which promotes the idea that we must all be "balanced" believers—strong in everything and gifted alike. *Cloning couldn't be further from God's will.* Though, I am certainly *not* saying that we *should not* do any of the things I just mentioned. I do, however, want to point out that God didn't create clones. We all have strengths, assignments, and gifts in the body of Christ and they differ from each other. *Diversity* is in every aspect of God's creation! Metron says that you have been endowed with a measured-out boundary (within you), which you live your life and serve God with.

You don't have to be *all* things to all men. In fact, you will never have real joy if you try!

Two: A metron is a place of authority and power.

The Greek word for authority is *exousia*. It is closely connected, conceptually, to the word *dunamis*, which is power, but it is different. *Exousia* means you have influence over something—a right or a privilege over something. Police officers are the best example of this. They have both power and authority—*dunamis* and *exousia*. Their badge is their *exousia*, and their gun is their *dunamis*.

In your metron, you are given authority, or *exousia*, to exert influence within the sphere given to you, but you also have power, or *dunamis*, from God, which gives life to your authority.

Three: A metron is a place of influence.

When you are operating in your metron—your measured place—you exert influence that comes from your authority. It may be influence over circumstances, influence over people, or influence from sharing your wisdom.

Operating within your metron is the place where you will be the most influential.

Four: A metron is a specific place within you where your spiritual gifts work.

According to 1 Corinthians 12, every believer is given gifts from God. Your metron, as we shall see, is where your gifts operate.

Your metron is where you give what you have, *not* what you don't have.

Bible Passages on Metrons

Now, let's discover the sure foundation for the metron concept in Scripture. The following passages contain some amazingly vital insight to understanding how God designed the body of Christ.

Romans 12:3-8 is a primary passage. In verse three, we are told that God has given to everyone a metron of faith. I have heard preachers misinterpret this passage by making metron (which is translated *measure*) about a *quantity* of faith. This passage does not speak of different quantities of faith but of distinctly different arenas or *metrons* of faith.

> For I say, through the grace given to me, to everyone who is among you, not to think of himself more highly than he ought to think, but to think soberly, as God has dealt to each one a measure [metron] of faith. For as we have many members in one body, but all the members do not have the same function, so we, being many, are one body in Christ, and individually members of one another. Having then gifts differing *according to the grace that is given to us*, let us use them: if prophecy, let us prophesy in proportion to our faith; or ministry, let us use it in our ministering; he who teaches, in teaching; he who exhorts, in exhortation; he who gives, with liberality; he who leads, with diligence; he who shows mercy, with cheerfulness. (Clarification and emphasis mine)

In the above passage, Paul challenges us not to think too highly of ourselves, but to think in terms of the boundaries of our metron. Then Paul goes on to talk about the different gifts which work in the metron environment.

In Ephesians 4:7, 11-13, and 16, Paul uses the word *metron* three times. In Romans 12, we are told that we are all given a *metron of faith,* but in this passage in Ephesians, it says we all have a *metron of grace*. I like to define grace as *God's ability to enable us to be who God has called us to be and to do what God has called us to do*. (Grace may include *God's Riches At Christ's Expense,* but it is far more.) Grace is God's enabling power in us.

Let's look at Ephesians 4:7, 11-13, and 16:

> But to each one of us grace was given according to the measure [metron] of Christ's gift...And He Himself gave some to be apostles, some prophets, some evangelists, and some pastors and teachers, [different metrons] for

> the equipping of the saints for the work of ministry, for the edifying of the body of Christ, till we all come to the unity of the faith and of the knowledge of the Son of God, to a perfect man, to the measure [metron] of the stature of the fullness of Christ...From whom the whole body fitly joined together and compacted by that which every joint supplies, according to the effectual working in the measure [metron] of every part makes increase of the body unto the edifying of itself in love. (Clarification mine)

In my opinion, these verses are the clearest way the Bible defines what church life is all about. Through this passage, we see that the growth of a church, into the fullness of Christ, happens when *every* metron is active and doing his or her part.

Second Corinthians 10:13, 15 contains another significant passage on metrons. Here Paul says that he will not operate outside of his metron. Thankfully, the Corinthian church was within his metron.

> We, however, will not boast beyond measure [metron], but within the limits of the sphere [metron] which God appointed us—a sphere [metron] which especially includes you...not boasting of things beyond measure [metron], that is, in other men's labors, but having hope, that as your faith is increased, we shall be greatly enlarged by you in our sphere. (Clarification mine)

Four Characteristics of Your Personal Metron

Through reading the following section, I believe you will experience a new freedom in your life as you discover your own personal metron(s). Below I have listed four characteristics that will help you discover your metron. As you read them, think about who you are and what you do with respect to each characteristic below.

When you are operating in your metron, you will:

One: Bear fruit or yield results.

When you are living, working, and operating in your metron, you will see positive results. It is the place where you are most productive. It is where "what you do" works, and it works well. For example, I am an organizational consultant. Through the years, I have learned what aspect of my consulting works and what doesn't. If you have a business that is going somewhere, I can help you reach your goals with excellence. I can spot loose ends in your business, problems in your communication systems, and I know when things are out of alignment with principles of productivity. But, conversely, if you want me to come into your business to strategize forward motion, expansion, or change management, I am not the guy you want. I have trouble moving forward in my own life, let alone trying to plot your future. I know how my metron works in business, and I know when I am outside of my metron. One aspect yields great results and the other not so much.

Two: Operate organically.

When you are in your metron, it is as if you have spiritual *software* in your brain. Naturally, you know *how* to do *what* you do—it comes organically, without stressful mental effort, exhaustive training, or figuring out. You must still learn and get better at what you do, by study and experience, but in your metron, you are not as dependent on other's knowledge to live or work, as you are outside your metron. You have a much more focused understanding, because you see what others don't. Your view is clear and obvious.

I have learned the difference between car mechanics who have learned their skill from a text book or course, and those who fix cars from a metron of understanding. This is not to say that they didn't become skillful from training and practice, but their knowledge simply strengthens *an innate ability*. I have found the same applies to physicians, marketing specialists, theologians, and countless other trades. I look for those who organically just *seem* to *know*. Generally, I think there's often an obvious difference.

Three: Gives you life.

Within your metron you are mentally and emotionally energized. Working in your metron is not "work." Your activity does not drain you or cause you to be stressed. This does not mean that operating in your metron is easy, devoid of hard work, or free from challenges. It just means, generally speaking, you get *life* when you are doing what you are designed to do. For example, Ruthie gets life out of taking meals to sick people or new mothers. She loves visiting widows and people in the hospital. She has a *feel* for the importance of doing these things and always feels productive in doing so. Many women don't enjoy these things. But stereotyping, at times, makes women feel as if something is wrong with them because they don't enjoy such things. The *metron* theology, when viewed as an overall concept (and not taken to silly extremes), gives people the freedom to be who God created them to be, to flow with who God is inside of them—and be okay *not to* live up to man's expectations.

I often say, within your metron you have *grace, but* outside of your metron, you have *stress*. Grace is wind at your back and stress is wind in your face! This is not an absolute statement, but it is a general truth that may help you discern your metron.

Four: Creates opportunities.

In your metron, you will follow what God is doing, instead of forcing something to happen. Opportunities will confront you, meaning, *when you are in your metron, supernatural things happen.* God goes before you, opening doors and paving your way. Over twenty years ago, I noticed God began opening doors for me to counsel and influence leaders. I would do a marriage seminar at a church and end up counseling the pastor and his wife. I had opportunities to speak to leaders. The churches I pastored drew leaders to join. They were top-heavy with leaders and potential leaders. I was often asked to advise influential pastors or business executives. My influence with leaders has grown over the past two decades, with very little effort on my own, doing little or nothing to open doors myself. The opportunities confront *me*, they give me life, they bear fruit, and I *intrinsically know* how to lead leaders.

METRON—AN INCREDIBLY VITAL SCRIPTURAL CONCEPT
Questions

1. Review the four-part definition of *metron* on pages 40-41 and the four characteristics of a metron on pages 44-46. Describe your own personal metron(s) in relationship to these definitions and characteristics.

2. Call out the metrons you see in others on your team.

3. If you are married, what is your spouse's metron and what is yours? How do they blend?

7

HOW TO DISCOVER YOUR METRON—AND OTHER'S

Getting Over the Straw—or *Not*!

The following story contains a lesson of great importance to the functioning of teams—yes, even marriage. If you have a position of authority over people this story will help you to discern if those you manage are in the right place or position. Of course, it may help you, too, if you are in a position or job where you are not producing the desired results.

Dave was a top-ranking marketer for a big radio station. He didn't sell ads to Joe's Pizzeria. He sold ads to Pepsi and GM. We met at a local restaurant for breakfast. After some chatting, I got to the point: "Dave," I began, "there are so many things in my life that make me feel as if I am on a treadmill—I huff and puff and burn all sorts of energy, and when I'm done, I'm in the same place I started." I gave Dave some examples and then, Dave taught me a lesson.

Tread-Milling: Going nowhere fast!

There in the restaurant, Dave came up with a spontaneous illustration to teach me a lesson. He took a straw and laid it down.

He then put four packets of sugar on the table. He placed the sugars a few inches from the straw and then told a story. At home, his wife told him they had a leaky faucet. He instructed her to get it fixed since he had a busy week at work. That evening, he came home from work and asked his wife if she had gotten the faucet fixed. She said she had called a plumber and left a message. At that point in the story, Dave put his finger on a packet and moved it a few centimeters toward the straw. The next day, he came home and again asked if she had gotten the faucet fixed, to which she replied, "I called again, and they said someone would call me back, but they never did." Dave then moved another packet a few centimeters toward the straw.

Dave continued the story, relating the efforts his wife took to get the faucet fixed. Each time he moved a sugar packet closer to the straw, the story climaxing at the end of the week, when the faucet still hadn't been fixed.

Dave explained, "Bruce, the straw represents the faucet being fixed. The packets are all the efforts my wife made, attempting to get the faucet fixed. The problem is that she never got over the straw. Bruce, I am successful because I do whatever I need to do to get over the straw, while others do most of their work beneath the straw. When I am talking to a potential customer, I don't piddle around with those who say *maybe*. I would rather have a *yes* or a *no* than waste my time waiting for someone to be indecisive. If I were in charge of getting the faucet fixed, I would not have left a message on an answering machine. I would not have waited to get a call back, and I would not have hired someone who would fit me in later next week. I would have called around until I got the results I wanted, and I probably would have had the faucet fixed in a day, with far less time wasted."

That meeting improved my life. I am always thinking about how to get over the straw, because in certain situations, I can process and plan things to death—on the treadmill. For instance, when I lived in Iowa, I was offered an incredible deal on an office to do my consulting and counseling ministry. The problem was, the office needed lots of work—redecorating, new carpet, and so on. On top of that, I didn't have any office equipment or supplies for the office. Weeks went by, with me staying beneath the straw, making little-to-no progress toward moving into my office.

My inability to furnish my office caused Ruthie frustration (7.8 on the Richter Magnitude Scale). Finally, she asked me if she could take over the project, to which I agreed. Within two weeks, Ruthie gathered people to donate time, equipment, carpeting, and everything else we needed. I even had paper clips in my drawer. I was now ready to go to a new level with my ministry in my new office.

Am I Deficient?

Was something wrong with me that I didn't get over the straw with the office? I will say that I am always working on being more proactive in places where I don't produce, but I was certainly not at fault because I didn't get over the straw. What happened with Ruthie and me is an example of how we all become productive by putting our gifts and strengths to work together. There are places I get over the straw where Ruthie never could, and she depends on me. The key is to learn each other's strengths (metrons) and team up to get over the straw. This is a lesson for any team.

A Tip for Managers

Perhaps my story about the sugar and straw rings a bell with an employee/volunteer you are responsible for. Is there someone you constantly have to motivate, tell what to do—someone who just doesn't seem to be able to get over the straw in their field, job or position, even though they have lots of passion, and a good heart? You may have them *mis*-located in your structure.

How Do I Discover My Metron?

The skill of focusing and living in the strength of one's metron is a journey. It is not something you discover by just going to a class. Here are three essentials to discovering your metron:

First, it takes time—as in, years of experience to discover what works and what doesn't. I get annoyed by some contemporary teachings, which encourage young people to discover what they are good at, and then tells them not to settle for anything less. There may be a strain of truth in that concept, but in reality, *discovering the place you fit the best, often comes through trial and testing, successes and failures.*

When I graduated from college, I knew I was called to the ministry. I had just married Ruthie and needed to provide, but I would only take a job where I could do ministry or at least memorize my verses. I ended up with a security job at the Hardware Show, guarding a locked door eight hours a day. I then graduated up to the US Post Office, sorting mail all day long for almost a decade of my life. It was the best ministry training I could have ever had, although, I wouldn't have thought that at first. During this time, I learned what I was and was not good at. I learned who I was and who I wasn't. What had seemed like unproductive years, at the time, enabled me to enter full-time ministry more equipped to accomplish what I was called to do.

Second, you will never fully see your own metron. Others will see what you can't see for yourself. This is partially the glue that God created to bring His body together. Ruthie sees in me potential that I don't see when I look in the mirror, and I see greatness in her that she wouldn't dare admit. I will talk about this in detail later, since this is an essential dynamic to the culture.

Third, metrons can change as we grow older and our life-focus changes. As you broaden your character, widen your experience, and rearrange your priorities in life, you may find yourself functioning in new realms of authority. One of the places I always said wasn't my metron is evangelism—my focus was always on strengthening believers and leaders. Now, God is birthing new strategies in my heart and a desire to reach the lost.

Why Understanding Metrons is Vital to Succeeding in the Culture

Call it the kingdom culture, call it teamwork, call it whatever—the blessed fruit of respecting metrons is unity, productivity, and synergy.

When we understand metrons, we have a foundation for tapping into the power of diversity, and we can use it to accomplish great things, instead of letting our differences divide us.

Different Kinds of People Who May Be on a Team

Just for fun, can you think of terms that describe the profiles of people you may end up with on a team? Here are just a few I came up with:

- Insensitive
- Nuts and bolts
- Half-empty cup
- Half-full cup
- Merciful
- Optimistic
- Pessimistic
- Logical
- Mystical
- Practical
- Spooky
- Processors
- Shoot-from-the-hip
- Administrative
- Controlling
- Safe
- Risk-takers
- Type A
- Type B
- High D
- High I
- Choleric
- Phlegmatic
- Talkers
- Listeners
- So heavenly minded, no earthly good
- So earthly minded, no heavenly good

We are all so different.

We all see life from a different vantage point.

We all have incredible insight and strength.

We all have incredible deficiencies.

Most of us don't totally know who we are.

Many of us are learning who we are.

We live to be our best and to help others be their best.

Great leaders blend all the different metrons, much like a musical conductor blends the various instruments in an orchestra.

All of this—a definite challenge! All of this—definitely glorious! Let's process this more from a very practical place.

How to Discover Your Metron— and Other's
Questions

1. Review the list under the subhead of *Different Kinds of People who may be on a Team* on page 53. What advice would you give on how to make diversity work positively within a kingdom culture?

2. On page 52, I mention that no one is designed to see his/her own metrons, but we learn dimensions of our metrons when others affirm our strengths. What are ways each person on a team can effectively help other team members to become their best?

3. In the book *Now, Discover Your Strengths*[1], authors Marcus Buckingham and Donald O. Clifton, PH. D. say: "*Each person's greatest room for growth is in the areas of his or her greatest strength.*" They declare that it is a flawed concept to think the greatest room for growth is in the areas of greatest weakness. How can you apply this nugget of truth for developing your metron(s)?

---

[1] Buckingham, Marcus and Donald O Clifton. *Now, Discover Your Strengths*. (New York: Gallup Press, 2013), 8.

8

MY METRON TUNNEL— YOUR METRON TUNNEL

Are You Right?

Here is one of the biggest challenges to maintaining a kingdom culture within a team: Because what you do in your metron brings results, and because it comes organically (you see and understand what other's don't), you think you are right! The problem is that others on your team also have a metron. And what they do, works, and in their metron, they understand what others don't. Yet, their viewpoint may be the opposite of yours. *So who is right?*

Truth has many vantage points!

Everyone views life through their own tunnel. And for the most part, *in our own tunnel*, we are right. This is often what causes division, separation, and divorce.

I am writing this on a Wednesday. On Sunday, something happened in church which some of us felt required some form of correction. At our Monday night elder's meeting, we put the issue on the floor. I won't bore you with the dynamics of the issue, but it was a perfect issue to bring out all the different metrons. There was unity, but there were also different opinions on what happened. The tunnels were obvious—I speak of tunnels positively—it's the way God made us. There were also different levels of passion, which were attached to different points of view—some were casual with their thoughts, with a small hint of *maybe I'm right.* A couple of others were more firm. There was one comment that had a tint of *my way is the right way* and could have had the tendency to shut the other tunnels down. The point of view expressed by this individual was very true, but it wasn't the total truth. This person saw the goal and the big picture and offered profound truth. But others saw *the people* within the big picture, those who were affected by this issue. Eventually, we put it all together for a mature approach and perspective in dealing with the problem.

Almost every time I come to my team with an idea or an initiative, it is refined and brought to greater maturity by my team. This does not mean that teamwork is always like making soup. At times, it can be (i.e. putting all the ingredients together to form an outcome). Sometimes, though, certain perspectives are unacceptable. At times, a perspective may be insensitive, come from a place of inexperience, not aligned with integrity, or out of sync with the vision of the team, and so forth. I, as a primary leader, have often put to rest my own opinions, realizing, as a result of the wisdom of the team, that there was a *more excellent way* than my idea.

Let's process a metron conflict in the book of Acts:

A Metron Conflict in the Bible and What *Could* Have Happened

Now in the church that was at Antioch there were certain prophets and teachers: Barnabas, Simeon who was called Niger, Lucius of Cyrene, Manaen who had been brought up with Herod the tetrarch, and Saul. As they ministered to the Lord and fasted, the Holy Spirit said,

> "Now separate to Me Barnabas and Saul for the work
> to which I have called them." Then, having fasted and

prayed, and laid their hands on them, they sent them away. (Acts 13:2-3)

Here Barnabas and Saul, whose name was changed to Paul, headed out for what is called their first missionary journey. They took with them a relative of Barnabas named John Mark. He had joined them in Acts 12:25. But for some poor reason or another, in Acts 13:13, John Mark bailed out: "Now when Paul and his party set sail from Paphos, they came to Perga in Pamphylia; and John, departing from them, returned to Jerusalem." We don't know why John Mark left—it could have been fear, Internet-porn addiction, a sweetie-pie back home, or maybe he missed his mommy. We can assume that the reason wasn't acceptable.

Then, in Acts 15, Paul and Barnabas decide to *again* go and check up on all the churches. An important fact in this story is that just as Saul's name was changed to Paul, Barnabas's original name was Joseph. But Acts 4:36 mentions that the apostles called him Barnabas, which means, *son of encouragement*. Barnabas had such an obvious metron of mercy and encouragement, the apostles decided to call him "The Encourager."

While discussing plans for this next missionary journey, Barnabas puts John Mark back on the table. Paul flips! He might have said something like, "Are you kidding, Barney? The kid exited stage-left when the going got tough, and you want him to go along? Which part of *dumb* don't you understand?"

"Paul, he realized his mistake. So you want to write him off? Where is the grace you teach everywhere you go?"

"Barney, the mission is dangerous, and the church needs us. We can't take the chance—and I'm not into adult babysitting!"

"Whoa! That was pungent! If John Mark doesn't go, then neither will I."

"You're kidding, right? You're going to deny the churches of your friendship and influence for the sake of this kid?"

"No John Mark, then no Barnabas either—and that's my final answer!" replied Barnabas.

And there arose a sharp disagreement, so that they separated from each other. Barnabas took Mark with him and sailed away to Cyprus, but Paul chose Silas and departed, having been commended by the brothers to the grace of the Lord. (Acts 15:39-40)

Two people, two opinions, two metrons. I have heard those from the pulpit speculate who was right and who was wrong, but my belief is that *they were both right*. They were both seeing truth from a different perspective. But I do believe that *they were both wrong*, also. I'm not saying they were wrong because they did not agree, nor am I saying they were wrong because they went separate ways. Notice in verse 39 it says there was *sharp contention* or *sharp disagreement*. In my opinion, had they valued each other's metrons, the disagreement wouldn't have been divisive.

The saints of the Bible weren't always saints.

Time and time again, I have seen unnecessary conflicts (like the one between Barnabas and Paul) happen in churches, in marriages, and in teams. It wasn't until God taught me about metrons, that I was able to put perspective to those conflicts. Since then, I have helped direct people to avoid relational separation in healthy ways. Diversity of personality, profile, values, and gifting, is brutal to manage, yet we are continually exhorted to *keep the unity of the Spirit in the bond of peace.*

The Last Chapter

The last chapter of this episode involving John Mark is amazing! In 2 Timothy 4:11, Paul writes, "Only Luke is with me. Get Mark [John Mark] and bring him with you, for he is useful to me for ministry." The words chosen here are part of an inspired text. Paul didn't just say to bring John Mark, but he noted, *"He is useful to me for ministry."*

Reconciliation is precious! I think we can confidently assume that Paul and Barnabas ended up friends again. Once again, Paul and John Mark were companions in ministry, and John Mark went on to pen the gospel of Mark.

So Who Was Right?

My perception is that John Mark needed both metrons. He needed "The Encourager," and he needed the stern, no-pity Paul to make him the man he became.

Years ago, Ruthie and I had a young friend who was constantly making poor choices. We spent much time with him. In certain seasons, it felt as if we were getting nowhere. One day, Ruthie and I had a disagreement, but not a conflict. She remarked, "He just needs love," to which I replied, "Love? He needs a healthy rebuke!" We realized that our friend needed both. *It takes all of us working together to support the fullness of truth!*

What God is doing in your life may seem outlandish, cruel, or you may feel as if His telephone line has you on hold. At times, you may feel as if you've failed. But I assure you, He is in the process of putting every circumstance in your life together to mature you and make you into the image of Christ.

"My little children, for whom I labor in birth again until Christ is formed in you" (Galatians 4:19).

Burnout: What Happens When You're *Not* Operating in Your Metron

It seems appropriate to mention the threat of burnout here, since it is a condition that commonly attacks people with vision, goals, and a heart of love. It is a disease that looms on the horizon waiting to attack.

Burnout is physical, emotional, or mental collapse caused by overwork or stress.

As I mentioned, we all have to do things outside of what gives us life, but burnout is a real threat if you are continually trying to engage *outside* of your metron.

I remember well when Ruthie commanded me to get off the floor: "There's life all around you. Wallow in death or get up and lead the life that is in your face!" At that, I stood up, gathered all the kids, and went to a park for the rest of the day.

It was a horrible time in my life. I had been the pastor of a church, which I had planted, for several years. The church was growing and thriving, but I was dying emotionally. I was victim of that common disease that attacks most pastors at some point or another: burnout.

Ruthie didn't always understand why I got out of pastoring: "You do such a good job!" she would say. "Why would you stop?" Back in those days, I didn't have the revelation of metrons, or I would have understood my burnout better. I used to fantasize, like an eagle fantasizes about gliding in the valley breezes, what it would be like to be free from pastoring (or for a less poetic comparison, like escaping from the prison *Château d'If*, for those of you who have seen the movie, *The Count of Monte Cristo*.) Pastoring was a prison! I literally hated it!

Today, I look back and realize that the burnout came about because I was operating primarily outside of my metron—what I did *worked*, but there was no life in doing it. For a long time, I thought I had to do it because I was successful at it. But, I later realized, if I would have listened to the voice of grace, I would have known that I didn't have the grace to pastor. My metron was elsewhere.

If you are living and working primarily outside of your metron, you can expect, at some point, to burn out!

A problem that will never go away is that there will always be more people who need your help than what you have time to give. Setting boundaries is a necessary challenge for those of us who desire to work heartily in the people-helping arena and, simultaneously, desire to experience the "rest" of the Lord. I often quote what I heard a friend preach: *There are enough hours in every day to do what God wants you to do.* Working in your metron is life-giving—overworking in it isn't.

Tyranny of the Urgent: A Concept That Helped Me Prosper

One of the culprits of burnout is the concept of *tyranny of the urgent,* which I learned from a book by the same name published in 1967 by Charles Hummel. Countless times, understanding this concept has helped me function more efficiently and respectfully. *Tyranny of the urgent* means: *Focusing on the things that call for immediate attention, at the expense of the things that are important.* It means that we let what is the most broken, what screams the loudest, and what burns the hottest, to keep us from doing what is really important. Tyranny is *short-term managing* that works against *long-term success.* It is called *tyranny* because operating under this principle causes the important foundations of your life or organization to deteriorate.

When you neglect the important, you create the urgent! Life always seems to tell the big, ol' lie that *there is too much to do.* The truth is that *there is enough time in every day to do what God desires for us to do!* It takes planning, praying, deciding, diligence, and wisdom to live above the tyranny of the urgent, but doing so is not optional for anyone desiring to succeed in long-term goals.

Are You On a Treadmill Headed Toward Burnout?

If you are burning tons of energy and seemingly getting nowhere, it may be time to get off the treadmill, before burnout sets in. You may need help doing so—a counselor, a consultant, a wise friend, or your spouse. Like any besetting disease—don't neglect the warning signs. God desires for every one of us to labor in the *rest of God.* That seems like an oxymoron, but it isn't. I believe we can all be effective, without being overcome by stress and burnout.

So how does a team work within each tunnel and stay one-hearted and in unity?

My Metron Tunnel— Your Metron Tunnel
Questions

1. I opened this chapter by making the statement: "Here is one of the biggest challenges to maintaining a kingdom culture within a team: Because what you do in your metron brings results and because it comes organically (you see and understand what others don't), you think you are right!" How can you practice humility within your team (with others who may also think they are right), especially when other's point of view differs from yours?

2. What are some measures and policies you can incorporate to prevent burnout in your team?

3. Are there any areas in your life (or on your team) where you are a victim of *the tyranny of the urgent*?

9

THE AMAZING PIE OR TEAMWORK IN GLORY!

Dissonance

Some of you know about dissonance as it relates to music. It's when non-harmonious musical tones clash. Multitudes of great songs—and more recently—multitudes of great *worship* songs use dissonance for incredible musical effects. *The Point of No Return* in *The Phantom of the Opera* is a well-known example of a song that uses dissonance to create emotion.

But dissonance is a broader term. It is *tension,* resulting from the meeting of two opposing elements. Sometimes dissonance is a negative term, but often it contains the opportunity for something of greater excellence.

I love musical dissonance and enjoy creating with dissonant musical patterns and chords. But another arena where I must work creatively with dissonance is in relationships. All relationships experience dissonance. Some dissonance can lead to divorce, church splits, chaos in businesses, and separation of friends. But just as in music, dissonance can be a catalyst for birthing greatness. It all has to do with what we do with it—how we manage it for positive purposes.

Productive and healthy teams experience dissonance. Without healthy dissonance, a team will be mediocre at best.

Using dissonant patterns in music is for the mature. Poor judgment using dissonance will sabotage any song. Likewise, directing dissonance in relationships is for the mature. Poor judgment will sabotage any team. Unfortunately, in my role as a mentor, counselor, and consultant, I am continually being called upon to help fix problems caused by less-than-brilliant attempts to control dissonance.

Healthy dissonance in music is glorious. Healthy dissonance in relationships is glorious. Kingdom cultures are dissonant—designed by God that way. Our goal, through the dissonance, is a masterpiece of harmony.

Mediocre leaders merely build teams; brilliant leaders build cultures!

The Glorious Pie

Often, when I am talking to and about teams, I talk about the pie. Understanding how a team functions effectively, when all the metrons are unique, is best illustrated by *the pie.*

The pie is the team. On one side of the pie, you have a piece of the pie that embraces one perspective, style, or gift. Directly opposite this piece, there is another piece, which has a completely different perspective, style, or gift. The different pieces represent the different metrons.

Usually, I use the illustration of the fellowship meal after a Sunday service. A section of the floor had just been mopped because a child spilled his punch. The custodian put up the "Careful, Wet Floor" stand. Jason comes through the line, ignores the sign and slips and falls—food flying all over the place. The question is: *What do the different metrons (or pieces of the pie) say, think, or do?* Josh is the prophet type—he looks at Jason on the floor and says, "*Didn't you read the sign, Dummy?*" On the direct opposite side of the pie is Katie,

Miss Mercy. She says, *"Oh you poor boy! Can I help you?"* Emily, a giver, says, *"Here, have some of my food!"* Arthur, the administrator, screams, *"You, get a mop! You, get a bucket!"* Who is most needed? In this case, I'd say, *every perspective is needed.*

Division or Provision?

I am not saying anything we don't know—we are all different—intentionally created that way by God. But despite the fact that most of us know this, in our brain, our diversity is still more of a *division* than *provision.*

Let's explore that more with a couple of examples: How many of you were ever made to feel guilty because you didn't get involved in a Christian political action picket? Did your non-involvement mean you were not concerned about our country? No! Did it mean others shouldn't do it? No! I avoid situations where I might be challenged to spontaneously *witness to the lost*. I do not have any desire (or calling) to go out on the city streets and preach or hand out salvation literature. Am I backslidden or apathetic? No. Is it wrong for others to do it? No. Am I not concerned for the lost? No. However, street witnessing is not my best application. I teach conferences and guess what? People find Jesus at my conferences all the time. I could not count all the people who have gotten saved during my public meetings. Years ago, a person in our fellowship, who loved community outreach, planned for the group to go Christmas caroling and give out food. I told Ruthie I wasn't going (at the expense of others in our fellowship thinking I was a crud-ball). I would have rather hung upside down in a cold barn with bats than have gone caroling. God wasn't offended, and I didn't repent.

I am not saying that we don't ever have to do things we don't want to do. We certainly do! All the time! The point I am making is that we are all different, and we don't all have to be *balanced believers*. We can prioritize what we are good at, or called to do, within our metrons. We don't have to feel guilty if we bow out of doing good things that we are not led by the Holy Spirit to do. If we understand the concept of the pie, we can understand how God made His body to function *INTER*-dependently.

House-Churching in Iowa

After pastoring a church for nine years, Ruthie and I were invited to buy a bed and breakfast in Iowa. I felt I needed a break from intense ministry and craved a business environment. Long story short—the B&B never came to pass, but the business deal didn't fall through until we had moved to Iowa. Fat chance of getting out of ministry! Within two weeks, we had a multitude of people showing up at our home to be ministered to. Ruthie and I were swamped with married couples needing help, wounded people needing hope, and so forth. The end result was what some referred to as a *house church*—which I was reluctant to label, since I didn't ask for the group, nor did I do anything to start the group. But alas, I was required to steward what God was doing.

Our group grew. We met on Sundays and Tuesdays. There was no position called "Pastor," we had no programs, took no offerings, had no bylaws, yet many people were transformed as a result of the group. The Spirit of God moved mightily, and we developed strong relationships.

As time went on, the different metrons emerged, each one seeing through his/her own metron tunnel:

- Word people – We need Bible study, we need to learn doctrine and God's ways!
- Evangelists – We are too self-focused! Nothing glorifies God like winning the lost for Christ!
- Eaters – We had breakfast together before every Sunday gathering. The Eaters are the ones who call the fellowship part real church, and nothing else seems as valuable.

They struggled when we transitioned from the informal socializing to the more formal part. (Ruthie, Ruthie, Ruthie!)
- World changers – Social justice people can't imagine how we simply focus on our own lives, while 90 percent of the world starves, human trafficking thrives, single moms can't pay their bills, etc.
- Prayer warriors – For these guys and gals, nothing trumps prayer. If we aren't praying, fasting, and warring in the Spirit, we aren't getting God's attention.
- Worshippers – Hey, by the way, the reason we were created is to bring glory to Him. Our first responsibility is to sing, praise, and worship before Him.
- Power people – Healing, miracles, and hearing from God is the way to go!

You get my point. In the midst of the many metrons, without the blessing of the kingdom culture, there is little hope for fulfilling the apostle Paul's challenge in Ephesians 4:3 to "keep the unity of the Spirit in the bond of peace." Learning the culture is imperative for anyone who desires to walk in the unity of the Spirit, in the midst of personal differences.

The good news is, *our differences make our teams great, productive, influential, and enable us to excel in amazing ways and to accomplish incredible feats.* Yet, historically, countless churches and movements split, tempered with animosity, simply because they didn't understand the beauty of metrons.

The truth is, we all place a different emphasis on various disciplines of the faith, *and we need every focus.* We are all called to be evangelists, we all need to study the Word of God, we were all created to worship and to do our part to oppose the evils of the world, and so forth. To be a disciple means we value every discipline, even though the "mix" may look different one from another.

Who Should Be The Speaker?

For one more example of metrons, let's look at public speakers. I speak at many conferences and seminars. In my years of doing this, I have seen organizers make the mistake of putting the wrong people behind the podium. Just because someone is knowledgeable, doesn't mean they have the metron to influence in a conference setting or even in a church setting. The metron of a college professor, who is great at teaching his class, may not work in another environment. Great pastors, who are effective at teaching weekly from the pulpit, may bomb at a conference. My primary metron is most effective in conferences or guest speaking. My gift does work well in a church environment. The altars are usually full at the end of my messages—but on a long-term basis, when I am speaking weekly, church services turn into high-intensity events. I could never see myself preaching through the book of Ephesians. Yet, discipling others requires the discipline of precept-upon-precept teaching, something I'm not inclined to do.

Black-and-white lines can rarely be drawn between metrons, but having this general knowledge of how metrons work, does help in placing people where they belong for the greatest productivity.

Metrons and a Full Church

Here is an example of a situation that could cause tension or triumph. A church I was a member of was growing rapidly. For quite some time, wisdom seemed to be screaming at the leaders that they needed to make more space to accommodate the growth. The options were: start multiple services, buy a bigger building, build a bigger building, or send out a portion of the congregation to plant a new church. A situation such as this has the potential to engage all the metrons—everyone looking through their own tunnel, confident that *their personal* perspective is also God's perspective. The relational people are afraid another service will divide the *community*. The idealists think a mega-church is opposed to God's kingdom plan. The high D people think getting a bigger church is just flowing with what God is doing. No matter what decision is made, someone will be disappointed; someone will think the wrong choice was made. Actually, both spouses in a marriage might have opposite opinions about what to do. In addition, in such a group, there are visionaries who are willing to take risks and non-visionaries, who do not like change. There may be those who are willing to take a risk financially, and the purists who will say, "No debt!" So in light of all this diversity, how in the world do we make decisions that *keep the unity of the Spirit in the bond of peace*? Let's continue!

The Amazing Pie or Teamwork in Glory!
Questions

1. Read the list included on pages 68-69 of the different kinds of people within a church. Which one are you most like? How can a church, with such diversity, keep the unity of the Spirit in the bond of peace (Ephesians 4:3)?

2. How does this metron list manifest in a business environment? What are some unique motivational mindsets one might encounter in a business?

3. As a team works within the concept of the "pie," wisdom is needed to know how to slice the pieces. Balancing each piece equally will *not* work. Sometimes one perspective is predominant for the task or vision, and other pieces tweak the outcome. How does a team navigate through decision-making with respect to all the pieces of the pie?

10

PRACTICAL WISDOM FOR THE TEAM

Let's continue on our journey and learn how to tap into the strength of diversity in a kingdom culture. To do so, let's go back to the pie and discover the practical pieces of how a team works.

- **Some decisions need one certain metron above another.** As a leader, I need to discern whose thought process (on my team) carries more weight. In terms of the pie, whose piece of the pie needs to be bigger? Not every metron is right for a given situation. Making a decision is not like a puzzle—taking all the metron pieces and putting them together into a final picture.

- **Every perspective may be needed, even if some pieces are small.** In the decision-making process, someone's metron may not be a major piece of the pie—it may be small—but nevertheless, he or she may still add a portion of wisdom needed to focus the decision more accurately.

- **The process has to be based on Ephesians 5:21,** "submitting yourselves one to another." This does *not* mean that individuals need to weaken their perspective when they believe they have a primary piece of the truth.

- **Primary leaders most often carry a bigger piece of the pie.** Someone has to be responsible for the primary vision. The gap between the primary leader and the second in charge is exponentially greater than the gap between the second in charge and the third in charge. Someone has to carry the primary weight of what happens on a team within an organization. Therefore, that person must carry a bigger piece of the pie.
- **The more crucial the decision to be made, the more *communicating* is necessary.** On most teams, you have those who *shoot from the hip*. They are risk takers and hate drudging out the details. On the other side of the pie are the *processors*. They want to make sure that there is no cause for failure and tend to process things to death. The team, as a whole, and the leader of the team, help create a healthy balance—allowing for enough processing yet, not too much. In some ways, risk is involved in every decision one makes. Some want everything figured out before anything is done, yet, others ignore important considerations in their forward motion.

Now, let's get into the nitty gritty of how a team, small or large, can relate productively, efficiently, and effectively, in the culture. *Here is where the proverbial rubber meets the road.*

Consensus Teams versus the Glory of Disagreement

A consensus team places itself under the rule: *Until we all agree, we do nothing.* I'm not saying that consensus teams never work. However, more often than not, they are a formula for going nowhere, staying safe, and missing opportunities. Many of these teams are based on the false assumption that disagreement is bad, and therefore, they miss the blessing of disagreement. So let's talk about disagreement on a team and how it thrives within the culture.

Life without disagreement is boring…well, healthy disagreement, that is. A team will thrive as it learns to manage disagreement, because disagreement is one of the most vital catalysts to uncovering incredible solutions and prolific creativity. *The less disagreement, the more mediocrity* may not be a totally true statement, but perhaps truer than most of us think.

Disagreement often drives a team to go deeper and solve root issues, which may never surface without disagreement. So whenever your team is in a place where you are locked because someone disagrees with the plan or the concept, you can either force what you think is right by shutting down the opposition, or you can ask the question: *Is there something else coming to the surface that doesn't meet the eye?* This is *not* to say you should always give place to disagreement. However, it is to say, you don't want to shut down disagreement too quickly or unwisely.

Typically, disagreement is viewed as a negative dynamic—and, quite often, it is! But *if* it is true that disagreement can be healthy and can be a catalyst to actualize your team's full potential, then *how does a team create an environment that nurtures and facilitates healthy, productive disagreement?*

Touch Not God's Anointed

I have been in leadership for several decades. I am well aware of the bad attitudes and the unacceptable methods of communication people employ when they offer *suggestions,* or when they disagree. I have been scathed by people who have disagreed with me or my decisions. What I would like to address is the pompous attitude of many leaders, who make themselves immune to disagreement or challenge.

One of the most flawed interpretations of Scripture I've ever heard is the common *mis*-application of a phrase in Psalm 105:15: "Do not touch my anointed ones." If you've been in church leadership, or perhaps *under* controlling church leadership, you've likely heard the phrase. Commonly, pastors and church leaders have adopted this command to apply to their position as a pastor, or some other position in the church, as a shield against people disagreeing with them. Sadly, they put themselves in an exalted place above others in the body of Christ.

Countless times in my life, I have seen sincere believers destroyed because they lovingly appealed to leaders to propose a better way, offer healthy disagreement, or to attempt to save the leader from the consequences of wrong actions. But these leaders teach that disagreement is dishonor. "Submit and shut up" defines this leadership protocol. I have seen leaders actually threatened by simple suggestions from those they lead. I have been connected to leaders who embrace this philosophy and are mentoring young leaders in the same perspective. In these environments, I suspect that I have been labeled as a weak leader, because I value constructive criticism or suggestions for improvement.

Let it be known, "Do not touch God's anointed" does not exclusively refer to pastors or positions in the church. It was in reference to God's people, Israel, and if it still applies, it refers to *all* of God's people. Young's Literal Translation of 1 John 2:20, 27 says, "And ye have an anointing from the Holy One, and have known all things…the anointing that ye did receive from him, in you it doth remain, and ye have no need that any one may teach you, but as the same anointing doth teach you concerning all, and is true, and is not a lie, and even as was taught you, ye shall remain in him." These two verses refer to *all* believers.

I do, however, heartily believe that *honor for authority* must be a core value in any organization—close to the top of the list. My previous comments were not for watering down respect, but for addressing false platforms (i.e. leaders not open to correction or suggestions).

But What If People Disrespectfully Disagree?

Again, I am addressing those who commonly misapply a verse

of Scripture to eliminate *healthy* disagreement. I do *not* propose that leaders need to be open to any crummy, disrespectful attitude that comes along. Wise leaders embrace *intelligent* challenges and are bettered from tapping into the wisdom of others.

There are many ways to deal with *UN*-healthy disagreement. Depending on the situation, I have handled disrespectful criticism several ways. The challenge is this: While I realize people who disagree may have a rotten attitude, what they say, or offer, may actually be helpful and true. At times, I have told people to postpone what they want to say until their approach is not tainted in the "wrath of man." Other times, people disagree because they only have a portion of the facts—they have one puzzle piece out of a 500-piece puzzle, but they think they see the whole picture. Lovingly, I try to challenge these people to *a more excellent way*, especially in situations where they are uninformed or misinformed. It is not wrong to embrace the honor of the position that you are assigned, but our challenge, as people in authority, is to respond to all disagreement within the walls of a kingdom culture and maintain the *servant-leadership* culture, which is what Jesus taught.

Are You Mature Enough to be on a Team?

If disagreement is healthy, and a team desires to achieve their full potential, then each player must be mature enough to sustain an environment in which *healthy* disagreement is invited and expected. This is necessary, but *not* easy!

At our church, we are presently doing a leadership internship. We invited eight people, who exhibited leadership qualities, to join our church-leadership team for one year. At every meeting, we have a leadership teaching or discussion. As I am writing this, last night is fresh on my mind. As a church, we are facing a very positive problem—more people than we have space for. As leaders, it is a critically important time for making right decisions about moving forward. In order to do this, we needed to hear the honest heart of everyone on our team. So I began the evening with a teaching on *how to sustain a safe environment in a kingdom culture.* If you are a primary leader of a team, I encourage you to facilitate the same discussion with your group. I facilitated a very similar discussion at a church I'll call DVC Church (I'll tell you about that next).

DVC Church Hits the Nail on the Head

Pastor Ezra asked me to teach for two weeks on one of my series called, *The Kingdom Culture.* When I began teaching on how teams work, I asked the church to respond to this question: *If you were on a team that was dealing with a sensitive issue, what would keep you from being honest about the way you feel?* There was no hesitation. Immediately, hands went up all over the congregation.

Their answers to this question revealed what hinders teams from achieving their greatest potential.

Here are several of their responses:
- Concerned others will think my answer is silly
- Concerned others might conclude I think *their* answer is silly, or I think my thought process is better than theirs
- Afraid my idea would be shut down and not considered
- Fear my idea is wrong, and I will influence in a negative direction
- Worried the one I disagreed with will be hurt or offended
- Insecure that my idea or comment may not be as good as someone else's

Other responses defined core attitudes or motives:
- Basic people-pleasing
- Fear of rejection
- It's easier *not* to be honest
- Don't feel safe

- Feel insignificant in a group
- Lack of confidence that I will be heard

After all the replies were in, I informed them there is a better way of teamwork than nurturing all these fear-based attitudes. In fact, every one of these reasons will inhibit the productivity of the team.

You can't be an effective leader if you are not willing to give all you've got! This means that your team, however large or small, needs everything that you have and know inside your mind and heart, within the delicate wisdom of proper timing.

A Safe Place: No Team Can Succeed Without It

I am currently on a team which meets regularly to discuss a certain aspect of the vision for a particular ministry initiative. Details of the focus are not important. What *is* important is that the greatest challenge a team such as this has is creating a *safe place* in order to be a productive team. I'm not sure this team gets this yet. After our last meeting, I had breakfast with Don, another man on this team. During the meeting, Don had respectfully and maturely expressed a contrary opinion about the way we were all headed. While eating eggs and pancakes, Don gave a disclaimer for himself: "I'm a person who doesn't want to be disrespectful. I am asked a question and I just honestly express what I think." After this meeting, someone kidded with Don, asking him if he was trying to get kicked off the team.

I replied to Don: "Eat a few bites, while I tell you the truth. You were honest and you communicated your opinion in a healthy way. But did you notice what happened? After you were bold enough to be honest, the whole meeting changed. You gave others permission to be honest and almost everyone expressed agreement with you. Had you not spoken, we would have gone down the wrong path or just wasted lots of time before we got on the right path."

A safe place is *an environment where honesty and disagreement do not have negative repercussions.*

Ruthie, Me, and the Secret of Teamwork

Ruthie and I are a team. On our team, I take a primary-leadership role, which thrills Ruthie. With that being said, I have always tried to facilitate a safe atmosphere in our marriage for honesty and mature disagreement. So has Ruthie. Because of this, I cannot begin to tell you how many problems we've avoided, how much time we've saved, how many problems we've solved, and how much improvement to our relationship we've experienced, all because of the power of honest teamwork—made possible in a *safe* environment. The fact that I am the head of our home does not deter Ruthie from being 100 percent who she is. And for her to be completely who she is designed to be, there must be a safe place for her to express herself—honestly, confidently, and without negative reprisal.

Nevertheless, contrary to our overall successes in teamwork, there have been problems we did not avoid and blessings we did not receive. At times, we failed to engage the kingdom culture in our relationship. We failed to adequately communicate, we neglected to hear each other's heart on a matter, we railroaded each other's agenda without consideration, and we held back our thoughts in fear of a defensive reaction. Our journey as a couple has been to minimize, or eliminate, unacceptable attitudes and practices which negate the power of the kingdom culture in our marriage. We try to create a safe place where we can both be who we are designed to be.

In order for any team to succeed in a kingdom culture and facilitate healthy disagreement, a *safe place* must be established.

Next, let's uncover attitudes and behaviors that will destroy the safe place in the kingdom culture (on any team, of any size).

Simon Cowell and Metrons

On June 11, 2002, a new obsession swept the nation when Fox

aired *American Idol* for the first time on television. Mimickers on other networks began creating look-alike competitions, of all sorts, largely following the general design unleashed by *American Idol.*

The show was a competition of young singers and singer-wannabes, hoping for a musical contract that would catapult them to fame. *American Idol* hit the 500-episodes mark at the beginning of 2015.

The winners were decided by three judges. One of the most notorious of the three is Simon Cowell, who created intentional controversy with his brutal honesty and his non-compliance to what seemed to be the general consensus of the audience and the other two judges.

One place where Simon came alive was when judging an audition of someone who lacked talent or singing ability. His comments were often nasty. He told competitors, in one way or another, not to *quit their day job*—he brashly told people, time and again, that they were *terrible.*

Though I was never much of a fan of *American Idol,* I did watch a few auditions and performances during those first couple of years. What always surprised me was how many of those who auditioned (who were clearly *not* endowed with a voice of distinction) argued with the judges. They responded with their own choice rebuttals of the judge's assessment. Their reactions provided Simon prime opportunities to humiliate them for believing they were better than they actually were.

My point is that every organization, or team, is eventually going to have the challenge of *what to do* with people who think they are good at something—when they are obviously not.

How Honest Should We Be?

When working with people who don't see themselves as they are, I certainly don't recommend becoming a disciple of Simon

Cowell. On the other hand, not being honest with people doesn't help them either, especially if a lack of honesty is simply to keep them from being hurt.

When we allow people on our team to stay in a "bubble" of false self-affirmation, the mission of the *whole* is challenged. Often, the victims are those who are not in the bubble. In a situation such as this, we need to ask the question: *How does the kingdom culture handle a situation in which someone esteems their ability more valuable than they actually are.*

I'll give a few tips when dealing with such an issue:
- *Be careful about confronting what really isn't a problem.* In other words, first, exemplify mercy, tolerance, and love which hides a multitude of sins. And also demonstrate a bit of perseverance.
- *If the issue does need confronting, wait for the proper timing to address the issue.* I often pray about the timing, asking God to open a door of opportunity, instead of barging through a door. When the Lord opens the door, I take my cue and enter. Be prepared to wait.
- *Address the issue with no more than two people at first.* Don't gang up on a person. Don't embarrass a person in front of a crowd.

In helping a person see what is NOT their strength, point out what *is* their strength. Call them forward. Be encouraging, even if the topic seems negative.

Follow up on their heart. Sometimes it takes days to process an episode of being corrected. Show you care with a follow up call or meeting.

Practical Wisdom for the Team
Questions

1. The five points at the beginning of this chapter, on pages 73-74, are essential to heathy teamwork. Review each one, answering the question: *How does each one of these points apply to the dynamics of my present team?*

2. Why is cultivating a safe place to disagree so important to effective decision-making within a team? Is your team a safe place to disagree? If not, why not? How can the team improve in this area?

3. Even in a safe place, do you hesitate to disagree? Why would anyone fail to give their differing opinion in a safe environment within a team?

11

Attitudes and Actions That Kill the Culture

In order to flourish in the kingdom culture, one must know what the kingdom culture is *not*! Certain dynamics that are very common on teams are *unacceptable* and work against the success of the culture. As previously mentioned, functioning in the kingdom culture is *not* for immature, self-centered people. Prospering in the culture requires that everyone behave in a godly fashion. Here are a few of the common (but unacceptable) devices that, if left unchecked, can cripple a team. Most of them are functions of bad attitudes or immature emotional responses.

Offendedness

Offendedness is getting hurt when others disagree with you, or when things don't go your way. People who are easily offended steal from the unity of the team. Such are self-centered people or those who do not know how to *"esteem others better than themselves"* (Philippians 2:3). An easily offended spouse can cripple a marriage. A propensity for being offended, while on the team, can throw a black cloud over the whole team and inhibit healthy proactivity.

Just today I had to discuss a situation in which someone on a particular team in our church was respectfully challenged on some things. This person became offended and refused to return phone calls or texts. Such behavior is unacceptable. This doesn't necessarily mean this individual is disqualified to continue on the team, but the culture requires that this person be called UP to a more excellent way of responding to a challenge or criticism.

Defensiveness

A defensive person is not easy to challenge. Their response is to defend their idea or agenda first, instead of considering the challenge, or taking personal responsibility for a mistake or misjudgment. Defensive people are often, and perhaps *usually,* those who are slow to admit wrongs and tend to blame others more quickly than seeing any error in their own thoughts or actions. It is not wrong in any way to defend a position or a thought process you may have, but *defensiveness* is when one is actually *self-*protecting, more than *truth-*protecting.

Passionating

I'm not sure it is an official word, but my term for being over-passionate is *passionating.* What can be wrong with passion? Passion is priceless—in its place. Everyone in a healthy culture needs passion and enthusiasm! *Enthusiasm generates life!* But passion can also work negatively in a kingdom culture. Often, it is used to quench opposition.

Lonnie's enthusiasm was generally appreciated, but when Lonnie shared his view in meetings, it was embellished with a passion that usually meant: *I have this incredible idea from the very inner chamber of God Almighty's heart! Imagine the great things that will happen if we do this!* Actually, Lonnie's undisciplined passion was manipulative—it set a platform that crippled others from challenging or disagreeing.

Ruthie is passionate. When she gets excited about something, it's like *how could there be another opinion?* This dynamic often resulted in me being *shut down*—her way was superior and mine was inferior. Early in our marriage, Ruthie's passion was like a tsunami, even in small decisions about where to go or how to do something. I was caught up in her agenda before I could even realize I may have a different opinion. One day, for some reason, we were talking about how some married people dominate their spouse. Ruthie asked, "Bruce, do I ever shut you down?" I answered, to her surprise, a clear *yes*—"Every now and then, when you get a thought process about how something is to be done, you railroad your way through, and don't even take the time to hear my heart or my opinion on the matter."

Ruthie didn't have a clue that she shut me down at times, so she asked me to point it out to her when she was doing it, so that she could become aware of it. In the next couple of days, Ruthie *passionately* shut me down three times, and each time, I pointed it out to her. She saw what she was doing and asked my forgiveness each time.

From then on, Ruthie has been very conscious of how her passion could have a tendency to dominate. She still gets passionate, but time and again, along with her passion, she'll catch herself and say, "*Bruce, this is just what I feel. What do you feel? I want to do what is right, not just have my way.*"

Shutdowns

A shutdown is when someone blocks someone else's opinion, or agenda, with strong statements (or when they don't allow another to fully share his/her thoughts or ideas). I just addressed shutdowns that are caused by unbridled passion, but shutdowns come in other boxes, too.

Gene felt shutdown when he shared his idea, because before any discussion could hit the floor to consider his idea, Ronnie interrupted him and went on a tangent about something Gene had said. Gene felt hung out to dry. The team hardly noticed that Gene was interrupted, therefore, he felt *shutdown*. The discussion never got back to Gene's ideas. Interrupting others, in any kind of discussion or conversation, shuts them down.

Shutdowns also happen when someone says something negative or critical about what someone else said—all this without hearing the complete facts attached to the comment or idea.

Apply this facetious example to other situations: I come home from work and see what Ruthie is cooking. I say, "Are we having that again?" Ruthie gets hurt. Tim comes over to mediate our conflict. I justify myself to Tim, "All I said was…!" Depending on the tone of voice and body language, think of all the different meanings of these simple words: *Are we having that again?* One is, "Yes! I love that!" Another is neutral. The third, which obviously happened in this example, is "Yuk! Not again!" This is a simple illustration of how manipulative shutdowns happen on a team. Tone of voice is subtle—or maybe it is just body language or a negative facial expression—all designed to shut someone else down.

Destructive comments are major *shutdowns* and culture killers. Manipulative sarcasm—"Miss know-it-all!" Cutting jokes—"My watch must be broken. It says you're on time for once!" Stereotyping—"You always support the underdog!" Angry expressions—"I rarely understand anything you say!" Or "That's ridiculous!" Attitudes, tone of voice, and body language can be as damaging as hurtful words. Let's bring all these things into subjection to Christ.

Detaching

A classic, immature behavior on a team is detachment. It's giving the cold shoulder or the silent treatment when things don't go your way. It goes like this, "If you don't like what I say, then you can do it without me!" It's called *adult pouting*, and it has no place on a mature team in the culture.

Fretting

Earlier in our marriage, I would share my dreams with Ruthie. Many of them were *way-out-there* ideas that were fun to dream about but not practical to pursue. Ruthie's reaction to me sharing my dreams was often *fretting*. She would panic and semi-fearfully tell me why such-and-such dream wouldn't work. I would tell her I was not planning on doing it, just dreaming aloud.

The result of Ruthie's fretting is that she ceased to become a safe place for me to dream, and so I kept my dreams to myself. One day, I mentioned to Ruthie that I didn't dream with her anymore. She was horrified! My dreams were a part of my heart, and she wanted to be in every place of my heart. I told her why I stopped sharing my dreams with her. She didn't realize that her fretting was causing me to keep this place of my heart from her. When she realized what she was doing, she dealt with the fretting, asked my forgiveness, and has since been a safe place for me to share my utterly bizarre dreams and ideas. It wasn't that her fretting was bad. She just didn't know that it was shutting me down. But also, in the process, I became more careful how I shared my dreams with her so that she wouldn't think *I'm right now going to sell everything and give it all to the poor.*

I have seen *fretting* sabotage good ideas in leadership teams. Fretters with a root of fear, or insecurity, will process a brain-storming idea as if it is a firm resolution to do something. Fretters must learn to be patient, ask questions, wait for details, and chill!

Dominating

Every team, even marriage, may have dominant, confident, outspoken individuals working with those who are meeker and reticent. The tendency, under normal circumstances, is for the team to lean toward the more dominant influences. The problem is that often those who are less forceful have thoughts and ideas every bit as valuable as the dominant ones. Healthy leadership on the team is able to balance the dominant with the not-so-dominant and bring out the best in each. A highly dominant person can create an atmosphere of fear among the others who find it threatening to challenge the dominant one.

Often, I have seen in teams a dominant dynamic that I call *Chairman-of-the-Board* syndrome. Not that I'm against having a chairman, but the dominating process goes like this: Josh comments, then Emily comments, then Josh comments, then Joseph comments, then Josh comments, then Amy comments, then Josh comments…and on and on. Josh likely is a dominant person who needs to steward his thoughts better. One wise man told me that for every one hundred good thoughts he gets, eighty are not to be verbalized.

Resisting Change

These folk aren't really seeing what is best for the mission. Quite often, they are locked in a fear of change. Frequently people who are *not* visionaries will be heard to say: *Why fix something that isn't broken?* This may be okay in its place. However, people who dislike change can be perpetuators of stagnation in any organization.

Politicking

I define *politicking* as: *an attempt to persuade or influence others behind the scenes—to agree with one's opinion, belief, or agenda.* Politicking is disloyal—it is manipulation, and it creates an unfair advantage in the team. Politicking is a cohort of gossip, often playing on people's emotion to get pity or support.

Overlooking

In my years of leading, team-building, and management, I would put a high degree of emphasis on *overlooking* as a major culture killer. It means that *you don't have a voice when you are supposed to have a voice.* If you have been a victim of being overlooked, you may call it *neglect* or *disregarding.* Perhaps you had insights, answers, or ideas, but were never given a voice—a chance to inject your piece.

Breaking Confidence

Any leader has to know the nature of confidentiality. Great damage is done to teams, and victims are created, when team members don't respect confidentiality. There are no clear lines to what is confidential and what is not, but a leader must know the difference. If you don't know, err on the side of being quiet until you find out if something is confidential or not. Inappropriately breaking a confidence is almost always a serious matter.

I will emphasize, *all of these dynamics will manifest on every team at some point or another,* but the goal is not to crush, or shutdown, those through whom these unacceptable attitudes emerge. But we need to be calling them UP to a more excellent way. The goal is to work towards a team that operates respectfully and selflessly.

Attitudes that Kill the Culture
Questions

1. Culture killers are often the status quo on teams. These unacceptable attitudes, actions, and reactions, will keep a team from healthy productivity. Which of the culture killers listed seemed most significant to you as you read through the list?

2. Were there any on the list that introduced a new thought process which you formerly had not considered?

3. No team or organization is free from culture killers erupting at any time, no matter how mature an organization is. What principles can be applied for dealing with culture killers as they manifest in a kingdom culture?

12

Ownership vs. Territorial—Becoming Familiar with the Difference

The concept of *ownership* is essential to a healthy team. It is a quality to admire in any employee, supervisor, leader, volunteer, or in a family—in every child. A person who takes ownership invests his or her whole heart into the vision, the task, the culture, or the mission at hand. When something can be described as *mine* it triggers responses of accountability that are not present from a position of *yours*.

Though ownership does not mean you literally *own* the business, job, or project—it means you perform as if you did. This rare and wonderful person takes every aspect of their job personally and is driven towards excellence. For example, Ruthie and I, and a few of our children, presently live in a rented home for many beneficial reasons. It is a nice but old farmhouse. Like all old homes, it requires a fair amount of maintenance. Though this home does not belong to Ruthie and me, we take care of it the same way we would if we owned it.

Managers in an organization may not even know the concept of ownership exists until they serendipitously hire someone with it—or accidentally hire someone without it. Suddenly, the sharp contrast between the good employees and the *great* employees—those who take ownership—become apparent. This newly-awakened manager now sees that the quality of ownership brings with it the kind of proactive and productive behaviors that gets things done, and done well, without the need for micro-management.

Workers and leaders who possess the quality of ownership are:
- Self-motivated—they don't need lots of time-wasting, unnecessary supervisory oversight, because they are driven to take a healthy initiative, without being told everything they need to do.
- Unwilling to rely on excuses for not being responsible.
- Trustworthy and faithful.
- Willing to go the extra mile. No! More than just *willing*—they GO the extra mile!
- Dedicated to excellence.

A strong sense of ownership drives a person to find ways to do things better, faster, and less expensively.

Ownership at Home

Dishes left in the sink again!
Stuff left on the steps and not taken upstairs where they belong!
Blankets left unfolded and not put away!
Not to mention, empty juice glasses on the floor!
Mom will do it, right? Wrong!
Kids, let's gather in the kitchen…I want to teach you about ownership. Part of your training for life is realizing that this home is yours, too. Everyone has a part in making life at home run smoothly. Unloading the dishwasher is *your* responsibility; picking up paper

falling on the floor is your job; changing the toilet paper roll after you use the last frame is your blessed duty. In this home, *all* things that need doing are not necessarily *Mom and Dad's job,* and you'll help—but only when asked. We all give and take—together.

One of My Best Lessons

One of the best lessons I ever taught my children was called, *The Worthy Servant: What Taking Ownership Looks Like.* I took it from Luke 10:17,

> So likewise you, when you have done all those things which you are commanded, say, "We are unprofitable servants. We have done what was our duty to do."

From the time our nine kids were little, we played games to help them learn what a *worthy servant* is. A worthy servant is one who does more than what they were asked to do and one who serves without being asked. For example, I would throw two books on the floor and ask one of the children to pick up the book I was pointing to. Their favorable response would be to pick up both books. Or I would purposely drop a book and not say anything. If one would pick it up without being asked, they got affirmation for being a worthy servant.

Though I have had my share of weaknesses in parenting, I see that every one of my children is, and has always been, exemplary in the work place. From the time they began working outside of the home, they have gotten rave reviews from their employers for their ownership character.

Nothing Less Than Ownership

Creating a kingdom culture requires the knowledge of ownership. *As leaders in the culture, we must guide those we lead to nothing less than a culture of ownership*—each individual giving their whole heart to the tasks before them and going the extra mile for the success of the mission.

Understandably, few individuals have been crafted into model team players in their life's journey. But when ownership is a clearly defined core value of an organization, we have a platform to call people *up* to the culture of ownership and train them in the values that accompany it.

A Poison Counterfeit—Territorialism

Watch and don't be deceived by a crafty, lurking villain disguised as *ownership,* but indeed, it is not!

Territorialism is a counterfeit of ownership. Sometimes it looks the same, but it never is. Often, it takes time and process to discover that someone is being territorial. A person who displays healthy ownership works *as if* he or she owns it, but a territorial person *takes control.* Territorial people protect their own department to the detriment of other departments. For a territorial worker, they borrow identity from the task they do, and therefore, suggestions and directives involving change threaten their control and, as a result, their identity. Territorial workers are quite often productive workers, but they poison the shared vision by creating separation, resisting authority, and protecting their own work from intruders who may alter what they are doing or how they are doing it. They work in a team, but only in as far as they have control over their sphere of responsibility.

Territorial people poison the culture. Because it often takes stern measures to manage a territorial worker, they make others, especially their authorities, appear controlling. That is because it takes healthy control to manage unhealthy control. That last sentence is worth reading again!

Territorial people usually see a cup "half empty" instead of "half full." They point out what is wrong, instead of seeing themselves as a catalyst for improvement.

How to Deal With a Territorial Team Member

First, leaders *must* confront territorialism. Territorial people will dig deep roots of disrespect in an organization if their unacceptable habits are not brought into subjection. The issue is that the root of their problem is not necessarily *how* they do things. The problem is that their self-protection and insecurity define *who they are*. Dealing with *what they do* can be, in a kingdom culture, an incredible opportunity to help territorial people from the inside—in the heart—so they don't feel the need to *borrow an identity* on the outside.

If addressing your concerns with them does not change the control issues, then territorial people must be relieved of their responsibilities, or *boundaries* must be created to protect the mission of the organization, and/or the other workers and leaders, who are victims of the territorial person.

Lacy worked for a large organization in the finance department. Her job was to give recommendations on decisions regarding money. Through the years, her duty to recommend evolved into *control and authority.* Her influence became so strong that even her supervisors walked in fear of making a decision that Lacy would not approve of. When a new department manager took over, he saw this problem, confronted it, and set new parameters on Lacy's control. At first Lacy was quite disgruntled, but everyone else was overjoyed that Lacy's territorial reign had ended. Lacy adjusted under the new authority and prospered under her original job description.

Edmond was trying to sell his business. People would visit the company, express an interest and then, never show up again. After a few months, Edmond spoke to a few of those who had shown an interest and found out that they all lost interest after they called the county zoning office. Edmond learned that the secretary, who had worked in the office for countless years, had become territorial. She gave a hard line about zoning possibilities to each caller, which drove them away. Edmond immediately contacted the county supervisor and scheduled a meeting. He found out much of what the secretary was communicating to the interested callers was tainted by her own agenda to reduce businesses in this neighborhood—actually, the same neighborhood where she lived. This secretary, apparently, had roots that penetrated into the realm of *control*.

Every team will be benefited by all members having a healthy sense of ownership. Ownership is based in strong character and is unselfish in all its ways!

Ownership vs. Territorial— Becoming Familiar with the Difference
Questions

1. In your own words, define what "healthy ownership" means (using as many adjectives as you can).

2. Do the same with the word "territorial."

3. Under the sub-head *One of My Best Lessons,* I discussed *The Worthy Servant.* How can you apply this concept to your culture?

4. Do you have any ideas on how to deal with a territorial team member, volunteer, or employee, which is not addressed in this book?

13

How Does Primary Leadership Fit Into a Team Culture?

Not that I am against giving positional names to define roles, but in theory, I am not a guy who gives a whole lot of clout to identity labels (e.g. Pastor, Vice-President, Head-Dude-In-Charge-Of...) as the basis for empowering people. In church life, especially, I believe much damage has been done by creating identities that we attach power and value to (superseding *internal* leadership character and authority). Yet, I believe a healthy perspective of leadership is a key to keeping all things aligned with God, truth, and a productive mission.

Defining What *Leader* Means

Where organizations, or teams, often waver is in failure to define the parameters of the primary leader. If a leader takes on more responsibility than what others think belongs to that position, that leader is in danger of being called controlling. If the opposite happens, he/she may be called weak, passive, or inept. There are different levels of vision, strength, responsibility, and tenacity in primary leaders—

everything from passive/weak to proactive/strong. There are also different environments that may require more leadership intensity than team intensity. If I can make an extreme statement that may need some balance, it is, *when it comes to strong leaders, the concept of balance may go flying out the door!*

Balance is virtuous, but it is not absolute! Jesus was not balanced in many areas of His influence. Balance is often perceived as *taming extremes,* or *bringing things outside the box into the box.* Balance is like finding a common denominator and throwing out the rest.

Balance, in its place, is awesome. It is virtuous, and we should seek it. But out of its place, it can be merely *safe* and *unproductive.* What I am saying is that there are times in leadership where balance can go too far. Great world changers are rarely (to never) *common denominators.* Extremes often need balanced, but balance isn't always a characteristic of functional leadership. One of the dangers of teamwork is that it can place something inside a box that needs to stay outside of the box. Healthy teams are not designed to replace *radical* leadership with *balanced leadership.* The stronger the leader—the stronger his vision, the stronger his grit, and the more radical is his behavior. Any leader who always does what everyone else thinks is right, is likely not much of a leader. This is *NOT* to say that leaders must be given the freedom to do whatever they want or think is right. This is where every leader needs to build trust within his/her team—trust based on character and on proven experience. A great leader is strong, but he/she is also a servant and one who is constantly working to better him/herself.

Another Breed of Primary Leader

Not all leaders are strong, up-front individuals, yet they are primary leaders. This style of leadership is usually not someone who is high D, or dominant, in the DISC Personality Profile. Some leaders are prone to stay in the back and push their team. They function brilliantly by extracting the vision out of their team. This model will look quite different than the model of a team led by leaders who, although being good team players, take a more primary leadership role. One model is not better than the other when both are functioning where they belong.

Some of you may be wondering if the kingdom culture, and the concept of teamwork, *waters down* strong primary leadership. This couldn't be further from the truth! A strategically chosen team is wind to a strong leader's back.

A leader must see what no one else sees. And though the team may refine or help direct the vision of the leader, or speak into the timing of the vision, the primary leader must be free to lead where he/she must go, in the timing of the Lord.

It should also be noted that different leadership environments, just like different leadership profiles, require a longer leash for the primary leader, than do other environments. An example of this is when a leader comes into a struggling organization, or one that is failing. He/she still needs a team, but in order to turn the organization around, the leader may have to be three quarters of the pie, or more, at least until the organization is back on track.

For many years, I worked at Abundant Living Ministries as a speaker and counselor. John Charles, the director, was a strong primary leader. He guarded the vision of the ministry, but he did it in a way that all of us, under his leadership, felt valued and significant. When we had a decision to make, we would brainstorm or cast in our own metrons of opinion. After an acceptable amount of discussion and input, John would process the feedback and make the decision. Though the decisions he made were not always the ones I would have made, I was always safe under his leadership. I knew that the one responsible for the primary vision had to carry the heaviest load. He, as the primary leader, had a sense for the direction of the ministry that the rest of us were not privy to. The ministry has enjoyed decades of success.

My point is that in his role as Director of Abundant Living, John was appropriately required to carry a bigger piece of the pie. Yet John still valued his team. For instance, I once came up with an idea for a unique training seminar that, looking back, was one I regretted suggesting. John gave deference to me and tried the seminar. It went okay, but we never hosted another one.

Teamwork is essential and beneficial in every level of leadership, but the team must clearly understand how much authority a primary leader has in relation to the team. This may vary according to the metron and experience of the leader and the mission of the team. Failure to bring this understanding will eventually result in unnecessary conflict from false expectations. Some visions are more effective when they are heavy on the "team" concept, and some are more effective when they are heavy on one person carrying the vision with the assistance of a team. Teams must understand how big a piece of the pie the primary leader has, because it will vary according to the factors stated above. Failure to do this will inevitably and eventually cause some measure of division.

Morgan Freeman Once

I absolutely love two movies about leadership, which Morgan Freeman stars in. Both illustrate how leadership works when extreme change or extreme proactivity is the agenda.

The first is *Lean on Me.* In this movie, based on a true story, Joe Clark (played by Morgan Freeman) is hired as principle of Eastside High School in Paterson, NJ. The school is plagued with drug abuse, failing academics, gang violence, and other extreme challenges. Clark's unorthodox methods anger school officials, parents, and teachers. He knows that Eastside will not survive without a radical program of discipline. However, in the process, he comes near to being ousted. But in doing so, he gains the respect of some of the teachers and students. The plot seems to build a case that Clark is extreme, arrogant, and indeed, *not* a team player, also one who fails to value the teachers. In the end, this ends up being a smokescreen when Clark's unprecedented success is finally unveiled. He recognized that the teachers were not equipped to make any marked change because they had become victims to the rebellious culture, instead of being catalysts for change. In the real-life story, Clark purportedly turned Eastside around and was acclaimed nationally for his tough-love approach.

At one point in the movie, a teacher, while handing in her resignation, vented to Clark in indignation for his harsh behavior and techniques. The background music and the atmosphere of the scene were designed to make you think Clark finally understood his evil ways. Even though I resonated with the teacher, agreeing that Clark was a bully, I watched this scenario play out and caught myself screaming on the inside: *No! Don't give in! The school needs your tenacity!* At that point, I had no idea how the movie would end.

The next day, Clark faces the whole school in the auditorium, obviously to ask forgiveness for his radical behavior. Instead, he announces that he has accepted the teacher's resignation, affirming his radical protocol for the school's transformation. Inside I shouted, *yes!*

This movie does not contradict what I've written about teamwork. It illustrates that leaders can't have those on their team who are opposing the vision they are laboring to bring to pass. The team must be supportive of the shared vision, or the vision will not come to pass.

Morgan Freeman Twice

In the second movie I want to bring up for discussion, *Invictus*, Freeman plays Nelson Mandela. It contains one of my favorite leadership quotes of all time. At one point in the movie, he had become the national leader of South Africa, and he was focused on breaking down barriers between the races. Upon the pleading of his aid, who is dogmatically telling him that his decision not to get rid of the Springboks (the South African rugby team) is a bad political move, Mandela replies, "In this instance the people are wrong, and as their elected leader, it is my job to show them that." She then pleads, "You are risking your future as our leader." Mandela answers: "The day I am afraid to do *that,* is the day I am no longer fit to lead!"

Primary Leadership or Servant Leadership

How could there be a book about the kingdom culture in leadership without addressing *servant leadership?* Many of the primary concepts which Jesus taught seem both oxymoronic and self-contradictory. Leading by serving seems in opposition to the natural mind—that's why you rarely see it modeled. It required Jesus blasting our natural mindsets with statements such as:

> Yet it shall not be so among you; but whoever desires to become great among you, let him be your servant. And whoever desires to be first among you, let him be your slave—just as the Son of Man did not come to be served, but to serve, and to give His life a ransom for many. (Matthew 20:26-28)

> But Jesus called them to Himself and said to them, "You know that those who are considered rulers over the Gentiles lord it over them, and their great ones exercise authority over them. Yet it shall not be so among you; but whoever desires to become great among you shall be your servant. And whoever of you desires to be first shall be slave of all." (Mark 10:42-44)

But not so among you; on the contrary, he who is greatest among you, let him be as the younger, and he who governs as he who serves. (Luke 22:26)

Let this mind be in you which was also in Christ Jesus, who, being in the form of God, did not consider it robbery to be equal with God, but made Himself of no reputation, taking the form of a bondservant, and coming in the likeness of men. And being found in appearance as a man, He humbled Himself and became obedient to the point of death, even the death of the cross. (Philippians 2:5-8)

...nor as being lords over those entrusted to you, but being examples to the flock. (1 Peter 5:3)

The Fallacy of Carrying My Briefcase to Teach You to Serve

I don't want to rile anybody up, but I do want to address a method that is commonly used by leaders to teach others how to be servant leaders—in exact opposition to what Jesus taught.

Pastor Ron was a gifted speaker and of significant influence. He arrived at the conference with his interns, whom he was teaching to be servant leaders. They carried his briefcase, fetched his Bible, and got him water to drink. His wish was their command.

I don't mind leaders who employ interns to help them, but I do challenge their idea if this is how they train them to be servant leaders. Read these verses and then I'll comment.

John 13:3-15 — Training His Disciples to Serve

Jesus, knowing that the Father had given all things into His hands, and that He had come from God and was going to God, rose from supper and laid aside His garments, took a towel and girded Himself. After that, He poured water into a basin and began to wash the disciples' feet, and to wipe them with the towel with which He was girded.

Then He came to Simon Peter. And Peter said to Him, "Lord, are You washing my feet?"

Jesus answered and said to him, "What I am doing you do not understand now, but you will know after this."

Peter said to Him, "You shall never wash my feet!"

Jesus answered him, "If I do not wash you, you have no part with Me."

Simon Peter said to Him, "Lord, not my feet only, but also my hands and my head!"

Jesus said to him, "He who is bathed needs only to wash his feet, but is completely clean; and you are clean, but not all of you." For He knew who would betray Him; therefore He said, "You are not all clean."

So when He had washed their feet, taken His garments, and sat down again, He said to them, "Do you know what I have done to you? You call Me Teacher and Lord, and you say well, for so I am. If I then, your Lord and Teacher, have washed your feet, you also ought to wash one another's feet. For I have given you an example, that you should do as I have done to you."

Jesus didn't sit down and say, "Hey, Boys, I'm going to teach you to serve. Here's a washcloth. Wash my feet." No, He said, "Hey, Boys, sit down here and I'm going to wash your feet." Peter reacted because it just didn't feel right to have Jesus take such a lowly position. But this awesome example Jesus set changed the apostles' lives.

You don't teach someone servant leadership by having them serve you. You do it by serving them. Follow their example, carry their briefcase, and get them a glass of water. Then, when they react because it feels out of place, tell them to do the same to others.

How Does Primary Leadership Fit Into a Team Culture?
Questions

1. How do you define *primary leader* in relation to your team or organization? How does the influence of team dynamics fit within primary leadership?

2. Under the sub-head *Morgan Freeman Twice,* discuss Mandela's response to the aid who challenged him with the following statement: "You are risking your future as our leader." To which Mandela answered, "The day I am afraid to do that, is the day I am no longer fit to lead."

3. How does primary leadership, which sets the course and protects the vision, flow with servant-hearted leadership?

14

STRONG CHARACTER— INGREDIENTS FOR EXCELLENCE IN THE CULTURE

In your quest to be productive, don't forget that the *foundation* of anything you do, will rest on the quality of the character you and your team demonstrate. I have been quite aware of how many business and ministry training courses ignore the emphasis on strong character development as a foundation for effective living and leading. There is no *spirituality* without foundational character. Too many organizational failures are unequivocally caused by decisions and behaviors that emerge from ignoring the principles of biblical character.

A few times now, I have mentioned that participating in a kingdom culture is not for the immature, self-centered, or those without quality character. Now let's chat about some essential values and principles that support the culture. Below are a few character-based behaviors that make a team, a business, a ministry, or a marriage healthy. I suggest using this list as a platform for discussion among your team.

- Flexibility
- Reliability
- Unselfishness
- Punctuality
- Decisiveness
- Deference
- Diligence
- Humility
- Hard-working
- Self-confidence
- Humor
- Compassion
- Patience
- Self-control
- Forgiveness
- Courage
- Faith
- Faithfulness

For Example

If you lived in Guatemala, an eight o'clock meeting may begin at 8:45. That's the culture; people adjust. I'm not saying it is functional or good—I am simply saying, *it is,* and people expect it. In the country where I live, the good ol' USA, excellence in leadership embraces the virtue of punctuality.

In a recent situation, Ruthie and I were meeting someone for the first time. We arrived at our meeting place a bit early. A few minutes before our meeting time, I got a text from the person we were meeting, letting me know he would be five minutes late. I said to Ruthie, "Many people would have considered five minutes tardiness within the limits of grace, and it probably is, but the fact that he informed me he would be a few minutes late, gives me a clue about this man's caliber."

Things happen. Traffic. Emergency phone calls. 911 bathroom calls. But I feel valued (that word again!) when someone who is late for a meeting with me, at least acknowledges their lateness. Otherwise, I think they simply didn't prioritize the importance of not wasting my time.

Strong Character—Ingredients for Excellence in the Culture
Questions

1. In the list of character traits on page 112, which are strengths in you and on your team, and which of the traits need improvement?

2. How does God build strong character in leaders?

3. Why is punctuality a virtue?

15

Research Proves the Good Guy *Doesn't* Finish Last

The Dilemma Adam Addresses

A subtle thought process exists in many organizational environments that needs to be exposed and confronted. It is the often subconscious idea that doing *what works* is more profitable than doing *what is right*. Within this idea, there are different levels and intensities of operating under this mentality—for some, doing *what works* is their primary *modus operandi*, while others revert to compromising and *doing what's right* only when the going gets hot. Some words for this are scamming, cheating, politicking, manipulating, avoiding, controlling, railroading, bowing, lying, forcing, and/or violating.

At times, I have wondered if operating in a kingdom culture is nice, yet a formula for losing, as in, *the good guy too often finishes last*. I have pondered quite a bit on the benefits of doing *what works* versus doing *what is right*, especially since I have seen that those who do *what works* often seem to prosper *at the expense of doing what is right*. Many business executives and pastors may scoff at the concepts in this book because they are accustomed to success outside of the values I have promoted. They may even view these principles as formulas for losers. For example, Jesus taught, "Whoever desires to be first..." Yet, I know of, and have been a part of Christian environments, where top down, hierarchal leadership is the *modus operandi,* and within that mode, they seem to have a semblance of success. Huge ministries and businesses have been built through techniques that violate most of what I teach in this book and what Jesus taught in the Bible. This book will *never* be found on their bookshelves.

But does their apparent success make their organization legitimate?

At some point, any leader who values the kingdom culture will likely be tempted to do what works over doing what is right. I sure have! Doing what works may involve *sweeping problems under the carpet,* and often, lousy choices can be *hidden* from anything or anyone that may cause confrontation. But one who is committed to the principles of the kingdom culture must be committed, *without compromise,* to those principles.

Many nonprofit organizations consume volunteers like wildfires consume trees. I've watched dictatorial leaderships build incredibly large organizations at the expense of human hearts. Based on my years of travel ministering, I would guess that nine out of ten of the members have some kind of personal horror story of abuse outside a kingdom culture.

But then I ran into Adam Grant!

Adam Grant Finds an Answer

I was blessed to hear about a book by Adam Grant called *Give and Take.* The book is a masterpiece of research. The brilliance of the book has been acclaimed by a host of reputable sources including the *Wall Street Journal* and the *Washington Post.* Grant is an organizational psychologist. At the time I am writing this, he is the youngest fulltime professor of the Wharton School of the University of Pennsylvania and has also been acclaimed as one of the most respected.

Grant addresses three categories of people in leadership: takers, matchers, and givers. *Takers* focus on extracting as much as possible from others, aimed at getting more than they give. They are self-promoters and expect credit for their accomplishments. *Matchers* aim to *balance* giving and taking. *Givers* are the exceptional kind of individuals who pour themselves into others, without expecting return—giving more than they get. Grant writes, "Givers are other-focused, paying more attention to what other people need from them… It involves a focus on acting in the interest of others, such as by giving help, providing mentoring, sharing credit, or making connections for others."

I could write a whole chapter on what Adam discovered in his extensive evaluation and research, but in summary, he proves that *it is better to give than to receive.* His collected data from multitudes of organizations proves that *cultures of honor and generosity really do work*—as in, the good guy does *not* finish last—in fact, more often, the good guy finishes on top. Takers may appear to finish on top, and perhaps sometimes do, but consistently, *their season of glory is short.* The success of givers may not appear immediately, but *they create a foundation of long-term success.* He illustrates this with fascinating real-life examples and thorough studies.

A hearty *thank you* to you, Adam Grant for showing the superiority of honorable business!

A Short Note from My Heart

Recently, I was telling Ruthie about a meeting I had with a professional person of significant influence, who is unselfishly giving lots of his time to me to help me increase my influence. As we pondered why this is happening, I said, "I think he feels valued by me, not just for what he does but for whom he is." Then I remarked in exasperation,

"Does anybody value people anymore?" Oh, I know some do, but honestly, even in Christian circles, takers and matchers dominate the ranks. We live in a self-centered society, and it is challenging to break out of that self-centered mentality as the norm.

Where are the givers?

I will basically address the following issue in more detail later in this book, but it is worth saying twice, and it fits well here: I can't tell you how often I have sat with someone and been overwhelmed by them talking about their own feelings, ideas, and accomplishments, almost addictively, without hardly a thought to consider me or my thoughts. I don't want to judge, but I can often discern where someone's heart is through conversations. Primarily, takers talk and givers listen. *Takers* give report of themselves, while *givers* are more concerned with others, engaging them in conversation and mutual dialogue. As I have told each one of my children multiple times, let *the person across the table from you speak the most words.*

Excellence vs. God-Excellence: A Big Difference

Adam's book, *Give and Take,* was not written from a *faith-based* perspective, so I would like to make a few comments about the big difference between *excellence* and *God-excellence.* A kingdom culture, by its very nature, is committed to excellence in all things: no sloppy communication; no failing to plan ahead; no half-baked pies; no getting only 80% of the project done before launching it; no neglecting conflict resolution—you get the point! *I value excellence as a primary value,* but as I have aged in wisdom, I have come to see a distinct difference between *excellence* and *God-excellence.* Excellence often tends to mean *doing things perfectly. God-excellence* means that *doing our best, while submitting to His guidance,* is superior to doing things flawlessly. So, *my verbiage* has shifted to promoting the idea of God-excellence over mere excellence. It looks and flows differently. The concept of excellence without the *God* attachment can breed unhealthy performance and unnecessary perfection. Someone may think that I am giving license to cut corners. *Indeed not!* (Or Biblically speaking, *"God forbid!"*) I am speaking of a more excellent way, one compatible with a kingdom culture, which ultimately yields more healthy results.

Understanding the difference between excellence and God-excellence will add grace to your culture, and it will diminish the tyranny of unreasonable performance standards. Let me illustrate.

Opening the Conference: My Conflict with God

Here is a short episode in my life where I transitioned from excellence to God-excellence.

They could have asked a host of world-renowned speakers who were members of their organization—one of the largest of its type of ministries in the world…so why did they ask *me* to be the opening speaker at the international-leadership conference? Though it wasn't an unfamiliar application for me, it was one that I was not going to slack on, especially since my calling is leading leaders and influencing influencers. I knew there would be high-profile leaders sitting in the audience listening to me set the tone for the entire conference.

I wasn't insecure and didn't feel out of place, but I did do my homework in preparation for this amazing opportunity. I was told I had one hour and that included prayer ministry at the end. It also included Ruthie speaking for ten minutes or so. When Ruthie and I went over my notes, she remarked, "You have way too much! You've got to delete some of this!" I knew she was right, but you know what it's like when every thought feels like divine droplets from the inner sanctums of Heaven; precious dew from the heart of the Holy Spirit—and absolutely necessary in order to develop the unified presentation!

That being said, at Ruthie's advice, I deleted a couple of lines (over twenty words!). But I still had too much. At the conference, about twenty minutes before I was to grace the stage, I was informed that

I had been reduced to forty-five minutes. Honestly, I almost crashed. I can't develop this message, have Ruthie share, and have a prayer time in forty-five minutes! Inside, my fragility surfaced. *God, why? Spiritual abuse from the Father! You hung a carrot of opportunity before me, now I'm going to look foolish!* I began desperately thinking about other teachings I could *whoop up* and substitute in a flash. I felt like John 11:35 (look it up)!

Then, in the midst of my desperation, a gentleman with an accent approached me and introduced himself as my translator. *What? Translator?* Now my time was cut in half—the little bit of time that was left. My amazing presentation was suddenly reduced to the equivalent of a half-page devotional out of *My Utmost for His Highest.* I freaked! But then...out of my inner man came that still small voice from the Holy Spirit, echoing the name *Gideon...Gideon...Gideon!* Suddenly, I knew that this was not about the "enticing words of man's wisdom," nor was it about my personal agenda.

As you may remember in the sixth chapter of Judges, Gideon was called to bring deliverance to Israel, but he was reduced from tens of thousands of warriors to a mere 300 to win the war. Now, here at the conference, I was reduced from tens of thousands of words to a mere 300—but immediately, after hearing that still, small voice, I came to rest. *I went from excellence to God-excellence!* There in that back row, minutes before my debut, I enthusiastically traded my agenda for God's, and it was well with my soul!

The Rest of the Story

I have never received a more positive response or seen more of an impact from a message than I did after that opening address. Years later, I meet people who were at that conference and still remember it. Some even remember in detail what I spoke about. I realize that what we call *excellence* is often *far* from what God calls excellence. Sometimes, God breaks our ideas of excellence. By breaking rules,

God is able to make sure that things go His way.

In the kingdom culture, people are expected to do their best. Keep in mind, that a person's best may not be the essence of perfection that you or someone else might do, because of their lack of experience, ability, or a host of other reasons. Yet it may be God-excellence to have somebody do something, even though the job may *not* be done with what we deem upmost perfection.

Paul, in 2 Corinthians 12, cried out to God to have the thorn in his flesh removed—likely so his ministry could thrive with more excellence. Verses 8-9 he said, "I pleaded with the Lord three times that it [the thorn in the flesh] might depart from me. And He said to me, 'My grace is sufficient for you, for My strength is made perfect in weakness'" (clarification mine). As a pastor, I know human resources may be limited, and it is better to have a willing soul take a post, who may not be totally qualified, rather than wait until "Mr. or Mrs. Perfect" comes along.

In my journey, I have learned, time and again, God doesn't always need things done without flaw. Instead, I believe, He does value us doing our *best*—in whatever we do.

Research Proves the Good Guy *Doesn't* Finish Last
Questions

1. What stood out the most to you from Adam Grant's research in his book *Give and Take*?

2. Do you understand the difference between excellence and God-excellence? Describe it in your own words.

3. Should a team make decisions based on what works or what is *right* to do? How does a team balance these two motivations?

Part Two

Four Absolute Principles of Management

In my years of organizational management, consultation, and research, I have concluded the four principles in the following chapters are where organizations *strive and struggle,* or *progress and prosper.*

Organizations and teams cannot reach their potential without prioritizing the below principles of organizational management.

A Solid Foundation

The simple things
are what we don't do
We want the profound
We want what's
new

The basics we miss,
the staples,
the core,
Somehow we don't value
small things
anymore

Wow me with insights
Enlighten a fact
Stretch me with principles
that I can enact

But don't give fundamentals
I've moved on, you know
I've got to solve problems
We've got to grow

Allow me to comment
Lend me your ear
The need for the basics,
will ne'er
disappear

Grow as you will
But if you forget
the backbone and base,
You will,
You will
regret!

In solving a problem,
check rudiments
first
fail in this step,
and you'll end up
submersed

Putting out fires,
disunity too
Fixing the broken,
will consume
what you do

Build with the values,
and never retreat
Nurture the principles
that conquer
defeat

Then grow and be stretched
As you build your creation
Keeping it strong
on an awesome
foundation.

16

THE FIRST D—DEFINITION

Where there are no standards, people make up their own! My friend, Rob Painter, often says, "You won't go to Hell for poor administration, but you *will* go through it! That's a mountain of truth in a thimble! The place where most failed organizations begin to slide is in failure to respect the most foundational, preliminary step: *Definition!*

Defining who you are and what your mission is, is not only an absolute essential from the beginning, but also a continuous process as you grow, develop, and change. Perhaps you were good at defining when you began, but you have slacked on the *re*-defining, a discipline that must be a regular habit and practice of every organization.

Defining and redefining (or even refining) takes time up front, and that's why it gets neglected—*I/we don't have the time.* What we really need to understand is defining and redefining actually *saves* time in the long run.

What to define depends on what kind of organization or team you are defining. For example, the first vital step to starting a business or a ministry is creating a *business plan,* where you set goals, and then define, think through, evaluate, process, and plan on how you will accomplish those goals. In a business plan, you define every dynamic and process that involves this fresh endeavor. It is a roadmap for success. Had many organizations, which ended up in failure, prepared a business plan, they may never have started the business at all. I have helped people with grandiose ideas format a business plan who, after considering the business plan, scrapped their idea, because they discovered the idea was neither practical nor wise. That is, after all the factors were taken into consideration.

The first step of the business plan (ministry plan or family plan) is defining your mission—what you are called to do and what you are NOT called to do. You might think defining your mission is a *no-brainer,* but astoundingly, many begin new endeavors by *shooting from the hip,* having no clear definition of their intended focus.

Here are just a few defining questions, some of which may apply to your team or organization:
- What is your mission and purpose?
- What are your visions or goals?
- How much time must you devote to this endeavor?
- How much help will you need?
- How are you different from other organizations in the same category as you?
- How much overhead expense will you have?
- How much will you have to charge to make a profit?
- How and where will you solicit contributions (nonprofit)?
- What is your *operating plan* that will get you where you want to go?
- What are the different roles or job descriptions?
- What are the limitations and boundaries?
- How does your team operate together?
- What are your core values?
- How do you make decisions?
- What are your policies?
- What are your procedures?

- How is your standard of excellence defined?
- What does your culture look and feel like?
- What kind of marketing will be the most effective? How much will it cost?
- What is your protocol for spending money?
- How often do we have meetings?
- What is the agenda and focus of our meetings?
- How do we hire, train?
- How do we promote people?
- How do we handle violations to policy?

The Guy Who Didn't Do His Homework

Justin was a friend of mine who opened a coffee shop along Main Street. The first week he was open, Ruthie and I visited his new business to support him and get a custom latte. I am very good at spotting things in businesses that are misaligned. I will often point out to Ruthie, or to one of the kids, a business that I don't believe is able to survive. I don't mean it as a curse. I can just spot critical danger signs within a business. Most of the time, my predictions come to pass. I actually feel bad for businesses that fail because they violate business wisdom.

At Justin's cafe, I noticed some things that seemed misaligned. I gave him the benefit of the doubt, assuming perhaps he was just behind in setting things in order. But every time I returned, my concern grew. Finally, I sat down with him and questioned him: "By the way Justin, how many coffees do you need to sell in a day to cover your overhead and to make a profit?" Justin confidently bluffed his way through, assuring me that he could easily make a profit. He was open to my questioning, so I asked more questions about his advertisement plan, his long term goals, etc. By the end of my chat with Justin, I realized that he had never done a business plan where he defined on paper everything he needed to do and everything that needed to happen in order to succeed in his business. He didn't even know how much profit he was making on a cup of coffee. I observed the business for a while. I never saw enough customers to make Justin's endeavor fly. It was obvious to me that it would not succeed.

Justin's cafe lasted only a couple of months and was a financial disaster. Had he defined his forward motion, he could have avoided the catastrophe, either realizing that his business idea would not work, or taking the right steps to make his business work.

Workers Want Clarity

Consistency in any organization is crucial. Have you ever sat down with someone at a restaurant, ordered the same thing, and yet your portion was significantly smaller than theirs? One worker puts six ounces of ice cream on a cone—the other worker, three. Good restaurants clearly define standards for consistency.

Policies and procedures take time, but they define how all are treated fairly and consistently. Job descriptions, chains of command, safety regulations, disciplinary procedures, and spending boundaries are just a few of the many things that need defined in any organization.

Without definition, you can expect confusion and frustration and often, hurt feelings from those who had different expectations from what you perceived.

Don't say, "We don't have the time to define," unless you want to also say, "We *have* the time to put out crisis fires!"

The First D—Definition
Questions

1. After reading this chapter, what areas does your team or organization need to define more clearly?

2. Discuss this statement: "Where there are no standards or defined expectations, people make up their own."

3. Do you agree with the following statement: "We don't have the time to define," unless you want to also say, "We *have* the time to put out crisis fires!" Why or why not?

17

THE SECOND D— DELEGATION

The second "D" stands for *delegation*. Delegation means *to shift the authority of decision making from one organizational level to a lower one*. Delegation is the only way to increase your effectiveness and productivity in an organization. The problem is that delegation alone doesn't do the job. Smart delegation is the real key.

The key to productivity and efficiency in NOT to do all the work, but it is to find the *right people* to do the *right work* for you.

Delegating gives value to people and taps into the power of synergy, a force that multiplies effectiveness and productivity! Synergy means that *the whole is greater than the sum of its parts*. If you can do "one" and I can do "one," together we can do "three." That's synergy—and that's what delegation is all about.

Deficient Delegation

Micro-managing is one of the characteristics of *not-so-smart* delegating. Generally, it is a dysfunction of delegating. So what is it?

Micromanaging is:
- Exerting excessive control over someone assigned to do a task.

- Putting too much attention on details.
- Unreasonably expecting someone to do a task "your way."
- Failing to encourage another to use their talents and strengths to accomplish a task.
- Exhibiting a lack of trust in the one to whom the task was delegated.

Many of us have had supervisors who have looked over our shoulders, diligently making sure the tasks are done according to his/her exact specs. Such supervision is often fear-based and is the fruit of someone with unhealthy control issues. Perhaps they make you feel as if *they can do it better!*

Yes, there are times when intense oversight is needed. Unskilled or untrained workers may need constant oversight, or tweaking, to become efficient in their role. Perhaps some, who may need to be over-managed, are out of place and need a change of delegation. Someone who is overextended with the tasks at hand may present a challenge. Leadership trainer, John Maxwell says that he surrounds himself with people that can do certain things better than he can and then releases them to do their job well.

A Big Delegation Mistake

One of the most common delegation mistakes is *making a decision in an area that someone else was delegated to oversee, without communicating to them.* This blunder is one of the most commonly made in organizations and rarely happens without someone being hurt. Unfortunately, I have made this mistake, too, many times and came out with mud on my face. I will share a few examples:

Carmelo was one of my very faithful and loyal elders at a church where I was pastor. He often encouraged me to schedule a marriage seminar to teach the church what Ruthie and I teach in our marriage conferences. In time, someone else approached me with the same vision of a marriage seminar, and I put a date on the calendar. After I planned the seminar, I announced it at an elder's meeting. Upon hearing the announcement, Carmelo, rather than stuffing his violation, perked up and very respectfully asked, "Why weren't the elders brought into this? And how come I didn't know, since I have often asked you to have a marriage seminar? Now it is scheduled on a date that I can't attend, and Karen and I would have loved to come."

Now, in some team environments, Carmelo may have been out of line. However, in our culture of teamwork, he wasn't. In fact, it was a very healthy challenge. I was caught on the spot—I had violated Carmelo and the elder team by bypassing them on something that was partly their responsibility to help decide. I apologized to Carmelo and the team. I told them that we were immediately scrapping the idea of the seminar, and we were going to start at the beginning with the whole idea. Carmelo was gracious, along with the other elders. We then accepted the plans we had already made but altered the date... and *we lived happily ever after.*

Jon got tired of raking the leaves of the big oak tree that shaded his back yard. Without discussing his decision with his wife or children, he chopped the tree down. His children and his wife were severely hurt by his decision. The tree was very special to them. They weren't upset just because Jon cut it down—they felt devalued because Jon didn't have the courtesy to communicate with them and hear their hearts before such an important decision was made.

Elsie loved her public relations job at the office, but the lack of essential communication often led her to think she was not valuable to her managers. She gave me an example: One time she found out through the grapevine that the office space where she had her public-relations meetings was going to be used for something else, and her meetings were going to be moved to another location. She was stunned that she wasn't told about the move, especially since the office was such an essential part of her job, and she was the primary user of the office. Nobody asked her opinion before the decision was made, nor did anyone think about all the meetings she had scheduled. Now she would have to notify all the people of the change. Had she not found out about the change, she and the others would have arrived at the wrong location. In addition, the new office did not adequately meet her needs. Finally, she asked one of the supervisors if it was true that the place where she had meetings was being moved. He said it was. She attempted to inquire, respectfully, why she hadn't been told. Her supervisor responded, "Don't you trust us?" This kind of breach of communication was common in her workplace and created a culture of mistrust and low morale company-wide.

If you are in charge in any way, always take the time to think about who may be affected by the decisions you make, and ask yourself if they would be valued if you informed them about your decision, or if they would be devalued if you didn't.

Before any decision is made, I've trained myself to think about whom the decision needs to be discussed with, confirmed with, or simply communicated to, before I move ahead. I still miss it, at times, but I have avoided many relational calamities by considering others.

The Second D—Delegation
Questions

1. From your experience, what are the difficulties that often arise which prevent healthy delegating?

2. What does *micromanaging* look like to you?

3. Why is it better to not give someone a responsibility, only to have to take it away from them later? In light of this, what principles can a leader follow that will help him/her avoid problematic delegating?

18

THE FIRST C—
COMMUNICATION

I dread writing this chapter—for one reason: How do I take a topic that has been talked about, taught, written about, emphasized, and included in organizational manuals over and over again, and then reaffirm its importance without being *blah blah*?

The big "C" is *communication*. Even though you've heard this topic before, *how do I convince you that the main breakdown in a healthy culture is still lack of, and ineffective, communication?*

Said another way:

If your team or organization is faltering, the first place you need to examine is your *culture of communication*.

Of course, I, too, could write a book on this topic, which could sit on a shelf, beside the hundreds of other books on the art of communication. However, my aim in this chapter is simply to challenge you to reevaluate the strength of your communication within your organization or team and to give you a few tips to consider in the process.

A healthy team thrives on healthy communication like the human body thrives on oxygen and water, and without it, it simply won't work!

The culture is hurt, people are violated, and visions are destroyed because of inadequate communication.

The culture grows, people are valued, and visions blossom because of healthy communication.

Healthy communication is a fruit of healthy, mature people who create healthy, mature teams.

Though this chapter could be a thick book itself, I trust I will be able to give you some fresh perspectives on how to maintain a healthy culture of communication, even though you may have heard dozens of teachings on it.

Ruthie's Startling Phone Conversation

"How often do you and the staff of your ministry get together to discuss problems and build relationships with each other?" Ruthie asked one of her friends who is in leadership at a ministry retreat center that was struggling over the lack of unity and relationship that exists on site.

"We don't!"

"What do you mean that *you don't?*"

"I mean we never have meetings to communicate, and we certainly never have fun together."

"Never?" Ruthie questioned again.

"Never! If there are problems, you just have to figure how to say things, and most of the time you don't know how it will turn out."

Ruthie and I know if we just let a week go by in our marriage without communicating with each other about life and circumstances, we would be behind and probably on different pages in major places. You can imagine the frustration in a large ministry that neglects relational and operational communication.

Every organization needs meetings. I hate too many meetings as much as anyone, but to be reactionary and not have meetings at all is dysfunctional—a formula for low morale and ineffectiveness.

Shoot-From-the-Hip Management

Many organizations attempt to operate through shoot-from-the-hip communication, which means, *they make decisions or execute an action in the impulse of the moment.* Literally, *shoot from the hip* means to fire a pistol from the hip, instead of raising it up to aim properly. Translated into life it means *to react to a situation without taking the necessary steps to make sure your focus is accurate.* Communication takes time, but there is no substitute for effective communication.

One of greatest quotes, without doubt, that has ever been spoken, and comes with different applications is: Don't say you don't have the time to do it, say you don't have the time *not* to do it! In terms of this chapter: Don't say you don't have time to communicate, say you don't have time *not* to communicate.

Notice that I am addressing *effective* communication. Great managers and healthy teams have learned the skills of communication that make their communication effective. Ineffective communication can waste lots of time treadmilling—lots of talk but ending up right where you began.

In any organization, communication must happen on every level. It can happen through email, staff meetings, or round tables at a conference center. Communication keeps everyone on the same team, going in the same direction, up to date on the processes, and a host of other essentials which makes a healthy organization or team.

Ruthie and I need daily meetings in order to stay on the same page. We get up early, hit the couch, pray, organize, strategize, talk, and listen. I'm writing this in the dentist office. On the half-hour drive here we discussed a travel issue Ruthie is facing, and she wanted me on the same page. Our marriage is healthy and one of the biggest reasons is that we communicate. *Quality communication is a bonding force at every level of teamwork and management.*

A Few Ways to Devalue Employees through Ineffective Communication:

- Don't respond to their phone calls or emails.
- Fail to transfer relevant information to those who need to receive it.
- Don't follow up on employee's suggestions or ideas (Even if the idea is not implemented, a response is still appropriate).
- Use harsh corrective words without giving the recipient a chance to respond.
- Use harsh corrective words in front of others.
- Convey vague expectations, which cause employees to feel like they don't measure up.
- Never give employees a chance to express feelings and perceptions in a safe, valued environment.
- Refuse to smile.
- Don't say thank you (If you are going to take me to task when I make a mistake, show me the courtesy of telling me when you think I am doing a good job).
- Be indirect—hint around instead of being honest about what needs to change or how you feel.
- Create an environment where workers have to figure out what they've done wrong.
- Don't give employees a voice to contribute to the *shared vision.*

A Few Ways to Value People through Effective Communication:

- Affirm them in private.
- Affirm them in front of others.
- Don't make decisions in areas delegated to others without consulting them first.
- Ask their opinion.

- Be consistent in the way you deal with people and situations.
- Stay in touch with the people and the issues your people are experiencing.
- Make the hard decisions, even in the face of controversy and rejection.
- Have regular performance reviews.
- Provide them with everything they need to know in order to do the best job they can.

Endless Communication

In my quest to become a good communicator at home, at work, with friends, and others, I find that perfect communication is illusive. Nobly, I try to do my best to improve and become more skilled, but, the human that I am, I still get caught in situations at times where I wish I had communicated better. The goal, therefore, is not to develop a culture that expects perfect communication, rather one that, as the Bible says, *hides a multitude of sins*. Nothing works better in a heavenly culture than an atmosphere of trust, mercy, and forgiveness—and from this standpoint: *Get really good at communicating!*

Practical Communication Challenges

Being effective at communicating is a challenge for me and for all of us. Amidst the jungle of emails—forwards, newsletters, non-essentials, and essentials—I often fail to respond to something that I should have.

While I am typing this section of the book, on my email is a lengthy message from a notable woman in our church. She is positively commenting on the present series which the senior pastor and I are teaching. I may not have to say much in reply, but valuing her means a simple gracious response with a *thank you* for the thoughts.

At one of the department's team leadership meetings the other evening, Sandy, the church administrator, mentioned she had sent out a request to everyone in the department. She was inquiring if there was anyone available to do a particular task at a special meeting we had put together at the last minute. She asked everyone to respond to her with a *yes* or a *no*. Nobody responded at all. Sandy didn't mention it, but she and her position were devalued by the non-response. By the time Sandy realized no one had responded, she had to scramble to find someone to do the job.

A Question for You, Mr. Leader

How often do people share their ideas on how to improve something in your organization and yet never receive a response back? It's easy to respond to good ideas that you are going to implement, but what if you don't like the idea? Is it better to ignore the fact that someone submitted an idea, or should you risk offending them by informing them that their idea is not the best fit? I would say honesty and straightforwardness shows you value people far more than neglecting them.

Perhaps you get one thousand comments a day and simply can't respond to all of them. That is not what I am addressing. I am addressing the cheap lack of communication that makes others feel *hung out to dry,* those who took a risk to help.

What about the negative emails criticizing something or complaining? I understand there are boundaries between you and certain people, which may require non-response, but if your non-response is because you don't value respectful confrontation or you feel threatened by complaints, I challenge you to a *more excellent way* in unison with a kingdom culture. Ignoring critical emails may or may not be the best approach. Perhaps the person is a gossip. Coming under the influence of gossip isn't wise either. Either way, there is a respectful and mature way to handle critique.

Lillian is a dear, older widow in the church. She wrote a critical email to me complaining that, as a church, we are not doing enough outreach. She provided a list of areas that were lacking. I know Lillian has a solid-gold heart and was worthy of a response. I thanked her for her comments, but then pointed out specifics about how individuals in the church were actually fulfilling the vision of what she thought we were lacking. I gracefully pointed out to her that if she was just looking at church programs (and she was), she would not see much. However, our church is not primarily about making *programs* to accomplish good things, but we are focused on releasing individuals to be lights set on a hill and live the gospel—and our people are doing just that. Her response to me was amazing. She repented for being critical and thanked me deeply for bringing her a godly perspective of what was truly happening in the church.

A Freebie on Emails: What Never to Use Email For

You can take this or leave it, but I'll throw it in here for free. I have a strong opinion about emails: Generally, not always, emails are *not* for the purpose of communicating gripes, offenses, rebukes, and so forth. First of all, tone of voice, body language, and eye contact are all missing, so one is left to his or her own imagination in guessing the true heart of the email. Second, responses to sensitive emails are inadequate and circumvent healthy dialogue. Emails are for two things: encouraging someone and communicating objective information. In the kingdom culture, if you have a criticism or correction of someone, I suggest you get on the phone with him or her to talk about it. Or better yet, speak with the individual face-to-face.

THE FIRST C—COMMUNICATION
Questions

1. On page 139, I say: "If your team or organization is faltering, the first place you need to examine is your culture of communication." What are practical ways your team can improve in the area of communication?

2. What stands out to you in the list under the subhead A Few Ways to Devalue Employees through Ineffective Communication on page 142? How about under the list on Ways to Value on pages 142-143?

3. One of the most difficult challenges leaders have in our age of email, and other online methods of communicating, is managing effective communication within the boundaries of healthy time management. What suggestions do you have for balancing these two important responsibilities?

19

THE SECOND C—
CONFRONTATION

You can work hard to create and maintain the kingdom culture in your organization or team, but if you don't apply what I'm about to address, your culture will fail. Yes, it will fail. I didn't say your team will fall apart, or your organization, or your ministry—but your "culture" will fail.

The principle that gives strength to the kingdom culture, and the glue that keeps it moving forward, is *confrontation*. I define confront as *to directly challenge or deal with a problem, or something out of alignment, with what is right, good, or best.*

I have met many passionate, godly leaders over my years. Far too often, I hear them say, *I don't like confrontation!* And for the most part, what they are all really saying is: *I don't DO confrontation.*

Concerning this, I have three pungent comments in response:

First, it is a rare breed that *enjoys* confrontation. When the subject comes up negatively, I usually say, *"Welcome to leadership!"*

Second, there is *no* effective leadership without healthy confrontation. Without healthy confrontation, your only choice is to learn to survive the best you can in an environment where things are out of alignment. You accept dysfunction as normal and attempt to succeed by dodging the problems and the poisons lurking beneath the surface. And when you live life this way, you can produce something that looks good, *but is never God's best.* I have said that one of the first lessons a new manager or leader must learn, is how to address performance or attitude issues in those he or she leads.

Third, *failure to confront is selfish.* When you put your own self-protection and emotional comfort above what is right, you are not walking in love, integrity, or godly character. When you fail to confront others, in some way or another, there is always a victim. Simply and absolutely, great leadership does not fail to address problems. Without confrontation, there is no kingdom culture.

The Beauty of Confrontation—An Incredible Bible Verse!

> A word fitly spoken is like apples of gold in pictures of silver. As an ornament of fine gold, so is the wise reprover upon an obedient ear. (Proverbs 25:12)

At times, confronting problems may produce division or arguments, but *the core purpose of effective confrontation is to create unity, healthy growth, stronger relationships, and more exciting teamwork.*

Unfortunately, the word *confrontation* carries a negative stigma. It brings to mind synonyms such as *division, fight, argument, separation,* and more. Because of this stigma, sometimes I substitute *addressing a problem* for *confrontation* in my conversations.

Passivity: A Plague That Disables Leaders

Passivity disables effective leadership. I looked up synonyms of disable and they all fit: dismantle, debilitate, deactivate, castrate, cripple, paralyze, immobilize. Passivity in a leader separates poor or mediocre leaders from great leaders. Passive leaders may have large organizations and appear effective, but no one reaches God's ultimate will or his / her potential through passive leadership.

I live in an amazing, and obviously God-blessed, county in Pennsylvania: Lancaster County. I couldn't count how many Bible-believing, God-fearing churches have over five hundred people in attendance on a Sunday morning in this one county—not that bigger is better, it's just an indication of how many here are attempting to live a biblical faith. There are regular young-adult gatherings all over the county. My children attend one with hundreds of people every Tuesday. Last month, I was a speaker at an international mission conference for a mission organization that has bases all over the world, and the leaders would joke about how many Lancaster County young people populate almost every outpost.

I begin by saying that God's hand is in this area in a mighty way! Ruthie and I are blessed to live here, but Lancaster County is not perfect. Across the Christian world, the problem of ineffective confrontation exists in businesses, churches, marriages, and teams of all sorts. But here in Lancaster, passivity is a major stronghold that puts a ceiling on some aspects of the county's spiritual prosperity. There may be some from Lancaster reading this that may argue with me on this point. However, I have found few leaders who are not aware that the problem exists. One demographic that is aware of this issue, as much as any other sector of people, are young adult girls. Time and time again, Ruthie and I hear young ladies vent, *where are the guys who will lead, who will actually pursue me?* They refer to the Lancaster County plague of passive guys.

I, of course, am *not* saying that passivity affects everyone in the county—it certainly does not. I am simply saying it is a significant issue in the mindset of this area.

When I was a professional counselor here in the county, Ruthie and I have often dealt with women who despised their husband's passivity. One woman screamed, "I wish he would tell me what I've done wrong and what I could do better, but he won't. He just sweeps everything under the carpet."

Once, in premarital counseling, a girl was hesitant about her relationship with her boyfriend. When we got to the heart of the issue, she expressed how she wanted a man who would help her to become better, not one who would always be nice. She wasn't sure he would love her enough to address her issues. (They are happily married now!)

Passivity is a major root issue behind failure to confront problems. The heart of passivity says, *I'd rather deal with the pain of the problem than the pain of confronting.* In so doing, one usually creates much more pain for themselves than the pain of confronting and solving a problem. Also, *when you don't confront an issue in another for whom you are responsible, you deter them from becoming a better person.*

Peacemaking vs. Peacekeeping: Virtue vs. Poison

Almost everywhere I am called to do conflict resolution or organizational consulting, I find it necessary to expose the difference between peacemaking and peacekeeping. When leaders click into the difference, often, they click into ways they have been peacekeepers instead of peacemakers. For, you see, peacemaking is a virtue, but peacekeeping is a poison. Peacemaking is healthy problem-solving and team-building, but peacekeeping undergirds the plague of passivity. Peacemakers do whatever they need to do to find real solutions and lasting conclusions—even if they have to cross brutal pain lines to get there, seemingly creating more unrest, on their way to peace. Peacekeepers find indirect solutions and sweep problems under the carpet without solving the real issues. They cover over problems or satisfy themselves with half solutions in order to get temporary traction. But, unfortunately, *whatever is stuffed away will manifest later in one form or another.*

Jesus said, "Blessed are the peacemakers, for they shall be called the sons of God" (Matthew 5:9). There is a world of difference between peacemaking and peacekeeping. The peacemaking can be complex and painful, but the peacekeeping avoids pain at any cost—even the pain that leads to lasting peace. Peacemaking is long-term and goes to the root of the heart, but peacekeeping is a short-term fix that only delays true peace. Peacemakers value honesty at any legitimate price, but peacekeepers don't express how they feel when what they feel may be controversial. Peacemakers are not satisfied until alignment is made with what is good and right, but peacekeepers conform to what is expected of them or what looks like peace on the surface.

Being safe, keeping things calm, sidestepping issues, and failing to come to total resolve can appear to be virtuous, but all this does is prevent the process of finding real solutions to issues and conflict.

The key to being a peacemaker is to value what God values and to be committed to establishing truth at any cost, in the timing of the Lord, as the Holy Spirit leads.

Peacekeeping is often rooted in the fear of being rejected, but peacemaking is rooted in true love. Obedience, strong character, and maturity make a person a peacemaker. Remember, true peace comes by tearing down lies, traditions and practices that don't work, and changing false belief structures.

Confrontation, to a peacemaker, is simply *loving others enough to tell them the truth, and bringing issues that are out of alignment, into alignment.*

Strong and Controlling or Weak and Compliant

The ideals I am addressing throughout this book are goals that we need to be working toward. The *how to*, *when to*, and *why to* of confrontation is the most delicate aspect of teamwork. On most teams, there will be those who are strongly opinionated. More than others, they tend to think they are right in their opinions. They are quick to confront, or address, things they disagree with. Perhaps they are not *controlling* in a bad way, nevertheless, their thought processes have much more impact. A good team can help strong people to see that truth exists, sometimes outside of their paradigm, and help them become more flexible, when needed.

Then there are individuals that will be much more hesitant to be confrontational, or honest, about what they feel. They are more *compliant.* They will rarely express their hurts, they will suck up offenses, and they will erect the necessary walls to protect themselves. They are often content to go either way. When we recognize that someone is in the category of avoiding conflict, we may need to "pursue their heart" more than others in order to find out what is going on inside of them. We may also need to help them develop the confidence to be honest, to address problems when necessary, and to become a *peacemaker* instead of a *peacekeeper.* A healthy culture is a learning environment!

Barnes & Noble Night

As an example of the positive nature of confrontation, I'll tell our *Barnes & Noble* story. Ruthie and I have had a fantastic relationship since day one. This is not to say that we lived without confrontation or disagreement. We have a healthy relationship largely *because OF* confrontation. When we lived in Iowa we would go to the mall and sit in a coffee shop at the *Barnes & Noble Bookstore.* There, in the midst of tons of people, we would hold hands and take turns asking each other these questions: *How can I be a better spouse? What can I do to better hold your heart, meet your needs, and value you?* Don't think sessions like that were always the easiest! They weren't. But, in public, we weren't going to *flip* on each other. There were times we pulled back our hands, or defended ourselves with "*Yeah, but I do this and that and this…and that!*" Those evenings at B&N tested the one major character trait we needed in order to create what we dreamed of in marriage—*humility*! But we had to work through our *self-centeredness* and conform to the kind of self-sacrificial love we desired for our marriage. Though we had to hash some things out, and quell the pride a bit, we always left the mall better people and better spouses because we addressed problem-issues in our marriage.

Positive Confrontation in Organizations

Listen to this amazing truth: Good people and good employees covet healthy correction. Yes, many reside in the camp of slow to learn, hard to correct, defensive when confronted, easily offended; but those of strong character *want* others to help them to become better people.

Stewart Liff gives an insightful perspective:

> One of the things that frustrates employees the most is when management does not deal with poor performers or people who misbehave. Employees despise working next to someone who doesn't pull their weight but earns the same salary, and bonus. When this happens, people conclude that management is not serious about outstanding performance because they are willing to tolerate poor performance. Every day that a poor performer sits on the job, does not make a meaningful contribution, and continues to get the same pay and benefits as the people who are working as hard as possible, it is going to rub [productive] employees the wrong way and set a bad tone.
>
> Always try and turn a poor-performing employee around...However, if the employee's performance is still unacceptable, deal with it; do not simply move them around. While undoubtedly there will be some short-term pain, the vast majority of employees will appreciate your reactions and respect you for doing the right thing and the

organization will profit in the long term. ²

As an organizational consultant, I have learned that for any organization with employees—*performance evaluations* (PE's) are imperative. PE's are designed to provide a positive way to address/confront negative things. PE's are a two-way street, not only giving the employer/manager/director the opportunity to address issues in a safe, positive way, but it gives the employee a chance to address issues regarding his/her assignment, which may be difficult or devaluing. One business consultant once said to me, "The worst thing a manager can do to an employee is not tell them what they are doing wrong." This is true in any kind of organization—business, church, nonprofit.

Notice these Bible verses:

Reproofs of correction are the way of life. (Proverbs 6:23)

Rebuke a wise man and he will love you. (Proverbs 9:8)

Give instruction to a wise man, and he will be still wiser. (Proverbs 9:9)

Now no chastening [correction] seems to be joyful for the present, but painful; nevertheless, afterward it yields the peaceable fruit of righteousness to those who have been trained by it. (Hebrews 12:11, clarification mine)

A wise man is wise because he is hungry to become a better person, and he does not view healthy, loving correction as a threat.

---

2   Liff, Stewart. "Improving Organizational Morale." Posted April 3, 2012. Association for Talent Development. https://www.td.org/Publications/Blogs/Human-Capital-Blog/2012/04/Improving-Organizational-Morale.

The Second C—Confrontation
Questions

1. What problems arise when issues are not addressed within a kingdom culture?

2. What are your feelings about the following statement: "If you are predisposed to avoid confrontation, you can never rise to your full leadership potential"?

3. How do you distinguish the difference between being a peacekeeper and being a peacemaker?

4. Review the Bible verses at the end of the chapter on page 154. What insights do have concerning the practical application of these verses in your team?

20

Essential Keys to Confrontation

A Positive Approach—
Showing Ways to Improve vs. Bad Boy, Bad Girl

Confrontation doesn't always mean that you approach someone from a *"you did something wrong"* standpoint. Most of the time, it is more effective to address someone with a *"let me show you some ways to improve,"* or *"let me show you a more excellent way."*

One of the best illustrations I have found to convey this truth came from *Reader's Digest* many years ago. It was a story about how one man disposed of his rubbish during the New York City sanitation strike in 1968. Daily he put his trash in a box and wrapped it in fancy paper and put a bow on it. He then put the box-wrapped-as-a-birthday-gift on the front seat of his car and let the window down. Every day his trash was gone. The moral of the story is: you can dispose of negative things in positive ways. I find that, when I must correct someone, if I first emphasize the positive, I get much more of a positive response to my corrections. Lesson: *Try putting a pretty bow on negative things!*

Wisdom on How to Begin Confrontation Meetings

Though not a universal approach by far, I have found the best way to approach any confrontation is to begin with questions. This engages a person's heart first and may convey important facts, bringing light to the confrontation. "Why don't you tell me about what happened or what was said?" This allows them to share their perspective and perhaps, give information that you didn't know. It may also defuse possible defensiveness. This approach has helped me, time and time again, to avoid saying insensitive things I didn't need to say, which came to light after hearing their perspective

The Voice of Timing

You may have a right perspective. There may be a clear need. But wise words at the wrong time will backfire. Being able to sense the right timing is a trait of the experienced and wise. To borrow the words of an Elvis song, *"Wise men say, only fools rush in!"* Waiting for the right timing may appear to be passive, but it also may be great wisdom. Younger leaders often are quicker to disrespect timing and exacerbate the problem. But, alas, the greatest teachers are the tough lessons of experience.

Choose Your Battles

Some battles don't need fought. Some battles are to fight in the future. Some problems, in time, work themselves out. To address some issues, you may have to wait until you have sufficient facts and evidence. Like the voice of timing, knowing which issues to address and which to wait on or leave alone, comes with experience, wisdom, and effective training.

Come to Conclusions

When addressing an issue which is out of alignment, focus on coming to a solution or a satisfactory conclusion. Don't end with indecision. The process of finding a solution may need more time, more research, or more communication, but always, in as much as possible, create a plan designed to come to a satisfactory conclusion. If a correction is given to an employee, set a follow-up time with the individual to assess progress and also to show you care.

Essential Keys to Confrontation
Questions

1. What are ways that confrontation can be a positive experience?

2. How can the wisdom of knowing the timing of when to confront be applied to your culture of confrontation?

3. Review the Bible verses about the rebuke at the end of the chapter on page 167. What insights do you have concerning the practical application of these verses in your team?

21

INDIRECT MANAGEMENT—
THE TOXIC ALTERNATIVE TO
HEALTHY CONFRONTATION

A couple times in earlier chapters, I referred to the process of dealing with issues indirectly as a problem in itself. In this section, I go into more detail, in that indirect management is a much-too-common trait of unhealthy leadership.

As I mentioned in a previous chapter on confrontation, most people dislike confrontation. I hear it all the time: *I don't enjoy confrontation.* My answer is: *Welcome to leadership!*

Leadership without confronting problems (in a healthy way) is simply *lame leadership,* or *lazy leadership;* whereas a culture of healthy correction, where issues are addressed maturely, is *laser leadership.* Healthy leadership requires courage, tenacity, and self-denial. *Indirect management* undermines these virtues by being cheap, weak, and self-focused.

But What is Indirect Management?

You have a problem with someone. You figure that dealing

directly with the problem or the person may involve pain. Why?
- The person may not agree with you.
- You may hurt his/her feelings.
- You may lose respect or creditability to that person.
- Others may not agree with you and you run the risk of losing their respect, too.

Therefore, to circumvent the pain and rejection you may incur as a result of addressing the problem *directly,* you concoct a plan to avoid the pain by coming up with an *indirect* plan to resolve the problem. In your mind, you convince yourself that this indirect plan will preserve your honor and prevent someone from being offended—and all the hornets stay in the nest.

The Default For Many Organizations

The process I just described is, unfortunately, the standard *modus operandi* in many organizations when dealing with problems and issues—eliminate a problem indirectly, instead of facing it head on. Indirect management, though, usually creates far more offense. The results are, at best, short-term fixes. I will not say that there are not legitimate times when dealing with a problem indirectly is the best way—there *are* times, but those are exceptions.

Unhealthy indirect management has many vices:
- It's not about what's best for another; it's about what's best for you. It's about protecting yourself, instead of doing with is right.
- Indirect schemes often put innocent people in place to do the dirty work. The responsibility to address the problem is passed to another, so the one who should bear the responsibility of dealing with the problem is "safe."
- Dealing with a problem indirectly leaves the person with the problem wondering, *"What happened?"* Whatever

lesson the person needed to learn is avoided.
- The energy and time people put into indirect management, most often, creates more pain than facing the issue head on.

The Road Less Traveled

During college I read M. Scott Peck's book, *The Road Less Traveled*. So, what is the *road less traveled*? It is the shortest, most direct pathway to resolving your problems. You should face problems head on. But time and again, people choose the path of least resistance. To illustrate: Watch TV—are you amazed by all the quick weight-loss schemes. I'm not saying some of them won't work, but what I will say is that the crave for quick weight-loss programs is based on the fact that people don't want to take *the road less traveled*. They want a process without pain, an indirect route, a *result* without the necessary suffering. And most of the time, they create more suffering for themselves than if they would simply eat less, exercise more, deny themselves, until their goal is reached.

An Illustration

Grace and Tara were close friends—at least Grace thought so—that is, until Tara began having "legitimate" excuses for not doing things together. Through the grapevine, Grace would later hear that Tara was hanging out with other people. Eventually, Grace concluded that there was a problem in their relationship, but she was clueless as to what it was.

The Problem

Tara enjoyed her friendship with Grace, but she lost "grace" in the relationship, because Tara felt as if Grace was dominating their relationship. Mostly, this was because Grace was more confident and aggressive, and Tara was somewhat timid and compliant. Grace out-talked Tara, and she out-decided what they were going to do or where they would go.

The Indirect Solution

Tara's solution was to avoid the pain of confrontation and deal with the problem indirectly—back off and find a new friend.

Here's What Happened

Because Tara was a people pleaser and missing the courage to address a relational issue with Grace, their relationship dissolved. Grace never found out why, and whenever she would ask Tara if anything was wrong, she simple told lies like, *I'm just so busy since school began!"*

Here's What Could Have Happened—or Should Have!

Let's pretend Tara had a strong character. When Tara realized she had lost "grace" for the way her relationship with Grace was heading, she caught herself drawing back. One night, she woke up bothered by the apparent wall now between Grace and her. She felt so sorry, because there were so many good aspects of their relationship, but she was weary of being inundated by Grace's aggressive nature. She thought that she would have to find a new friend to take Grace's place. But the more she processed that decision, the more she realized that backing off from the relationship, without trying to help Grace see her issues, would be selfish and unfair to Grace. Though she struggled with the risk of hurting Grace, she knew that it was right to have a mature talk with her about how her actions were negatively affecting the relationship.

She decided to address the problem directly.

Grace and Tara are still good friends, but only because now they are better people. Why? Tara maturely addressed how Grace *shuts her down* and dominates conversation. Grace was stunned. She had no idea she came across that way. She even concluded that she was probably affecting other friendships the same way. Grace asked Tara to walk with her in her journey to be more conscious of the *rules of relationships*. Tara agreed. Grace changed. Their friendship continues to flourish after many years.

Again, I repeat, I *am* aware that there are exceptions where an indirect solution is the right solution, but predominantly, it is a violation of love, trust, leadership integrity, and valiant character. The title of a book by David Augsburger says much: *Caring Enough to Confront*.

Years ago, I was the sole instrumentalist for the song service at a church I attended. It was in the early years of my piano playing, and I was not very versatile yet in my accompaniment. The pastor's indirect solution, rather than directly talking to me about the need to upgrade the quality of our worship time, was to start the worship service five minutes early one Sunday. He had invited someone with a guitar up to the stage to accompany him in his song leading. Never a word was spoken to me—I had to read between the lines—I was out… and wounded.

In another example, Fritz had an assistant foreman position in a construction company. His skill at construction was inadequate, but instead of talking with Fritz directly, the solution of the managers was to concoct a reason to eliminate his position. Fritz never understood what really happened until he got another job. He then heard that someone else at his former place of employment got the same position he had—the one that was temporarily eliminated.

I could give you many more examples and likely bore you, but if you are in any form of leadership, you likely know the temptation that occurs when something volatile (under your authority) goes awry—*find a safe way to avoid offense, controversy, or pain, by creating an indirect fix*. Maybe, every once in a blue moon, that may be okay depending on the situation, but the protocol is, when the time is right, strap on your love, your authority, and your duty, and address the problem professionally, sensitively, trusting God to go before and prepare the way.

The Rebuke in a Fragile Culture

I was sitting with Ruthie in the pew of the small Caribbean island church, waiting to be introduced as the visiting speaker of the morning. Out of the blue, I received, what I often call, *a download from God*. It is as if God takes over my thoughts and causes me to perceive truth outside of my own box. The result is that I end up understanding something I previously wouldn't have.

What God showed me had nothing to do with the morning's message, but it had everything to do with a crisis situation Ruthie and I were involved in.

Downloads such as this often come in a flash, perhaps a few seconds, where the clouds are opened letting the light shine through. If you asked me, *"What did God show you?"* it would be difficult to put into words, but here goes:

The word *rebuke* appears in the Bible many times in both the Old and the New Testament. What the Lord showed me was that a large delegation of our culture does not have an understanding for the principle of *rebuke*. When I refer to a rebuke, I'm not talking about *angry, unhealthy venting and screaming* of something you didn't like. I'm talking about direct correction done with maturity and love.

It's not as if what God showed me was a new thought. I had felt the same thing for quite some time—there's a prevailing mindset which demands that correcting others always be done in a delicate and encouraging way, so that people don't feel *hurt*. I, too, joined that camp, largely because, at times in my life, I had been too harsh in an unhealthy way and lost trust in myself. I also perceived that many people had been victimized by rebukes that were not given in love—perhaps out of defensiveness and control. I believe in gentle, encouraging confrontation as the primary default of confronting—but I also believe there is a time and place for *the rebuke,* and a rebuke speaks differently than a *correction* or merely *addressing an issue.*

Rebuke is defined as, "Express sharp disapproval of someone's behavior or actions; to reprimand; to forbid." The biblical words convey the idea of both the *authority* of the person who is rebuking another, and *compliance* from the one being rebuked.

Often, in the context of leadership, in our wounded society, someone offering a healthy rebuke (again, a healthy one!) to someone will often end up the bad person, the mad person, the mean person, the controlling person, and so forth. So, to babysit the fragile emotions of many in our culture, some have scrapped the virtue of the rebuke, and resigned themselves to be the bad guy if they happen to need to rebuke someone.

I will close this section with a few of the many Bible verses on the subject of *rebuking:*

> Open rebuke is better than love carefully concealed. Faithful are the wounds of a friend. (Proverbs 27:5-6)

> Speak these things. Exhort and rebuke with all authority. Let no one despise you. (Titus 2:15)

> Do not correct a scoffer, lest he hate you; Rebuke a wise man, and he will love you. (Proverbs 9:8)

> Rebuke is more effective for a wise man than a hundred blows on a fool. (Proverbs 17:10)

> If your brother sins against you, rebuke him; and if he repents, forgive him. (Luke 17:3)

Indirect Management—The Toxic Alternative to Healthy Confrontation
Questions

1. How does a team, any size—married couple or leadership team at church, etc.—process the temptation to deal with a problem indirectly?

2. What are the virtues of *not* dealing with a problem indirectly?

3. What does the *wisdom of timing* say in respect to dealing directly with an alignment problem within a team or in an individual?

4. Can you recall a time you felt violated by someone who indirectly dealt with something they didn't value in your life?

Part Three

INFUSING LIFE INTO YOUR CULTURE

The next three chapters are about creating and maintaining the life-giving spirit of the kingdom culture—the grace, the glory, and the beauty. The first chapter in this section leads to the next, and then both support the third chapter. The concepts in this part of the book will take your kingdom culture—from bland to mediocre, from mediocre to great!

> What you see when you look at me,
> What I view when I look at you,
> Is only that which we have discovered.
>
> There is more, much more,
> That must be recovered.
> Down inside, though very deep,
> Are hidden sheaves that we must reap.
>
> But I can't see
> What's in my heart, or yours—
> You only see in part.

But I see greatness in your soul,
And you see what will make me
Whole.

So past your surface, I'll see through,
And this, my friend, I promise you:
I'll listen closely as you tell
What's deep
What's deep
Within my well.

22

THE GOD-MIRROR

What you've been saved for, is greater than what you've been saved from.
    —Dale Mast, Pastor of Destiny Christian Fellowship,
                                                    Dover, DE

At the church I attend, *the God-Mirror* is standard terminology. It became a theme for my ministry and is a core value for my life. I hope it becomes standard terminology in your culture, too.

The God-mirror theme is what creates a major part of the healthy life in the kingdom culture.

Honestly, I passionately believe that training your church, or your team, to understand this concept will dynamically improve the atmosphere of your relational culture.

So, What Is A God-Mirror?

I call this teaching *Two Mirrors: Identifying Your Identity*. It begins with this profound truth: *Your greatest challenge in life is what you think about yourself.* Satan's primary strategy to defeat believers is *identity theft*. He attempts to steal a believer's sense of worth to God and to others, or to tempt them to find their worth in something external. Let's discover how an understanding of the God-mirror defeats identity theft and builds the kingdom culture.

Every person has two mirrors. I call the first one *the natural mirror,* or the *me-mirror.* It's the one you look into when you comb your hair. This mirror is where most people live, move, and possess their being—even believers. Many people don't even know that there is another mirror—the *God-Mirror.* In this mirror lies the key to abundance, increase, joy, and self-worth. It is also the foundation to a thriving life, an abundant marriage, and a divine purpose in life.

None of these things will peer back at you from the natural mirror. Many people never look into their God- mirror, and some may only get a few glimpses of it in their lifetime. Actually, fewer abide (or think) in it, because its existence is elusive. Then there are those who know it exists but scream: *I can't get there!*

I often say that *God's redemption for His people is simply transitioning from the natural mirror to the God-mirror.* It is what the process of salvation is all about! It is the renewing of the mind, according to Ephesians 4:22-24, that transitions us from living from the vantage point of the old man, to the vantage point of the new man, from *old things* to the *new creature in Christ Jesus.*

Positionally, we are already a new man, or a new creature, in Christ Jesus. That being said, *now* we must allow God to renew our minds so that we can live and think as a new man—we can live and think through the God-mirror.

No one can live victoriously through the natural mirror!
No one can fail to live victoriously through the God-mirror!

Mirror one, the natural mirror, is the one we are born with. Mirror two, the God-mirror, is the one we are born *again* with. Sadly, many do not transition.

About the natural mirror:
- Defined by others (parents, peers, etc.)
- Defined by circumstances (successes, failures, wounds, trauma)
- Defined by self-talk (how you figured out who you are)
- Defined by other's expectations (what do I live up to and not live up to)
- Defined by society (what the world considers valuable)

About the God-mirror:
- Defined by God's Word
- Defined by inner value
- Defined by the Spirit's expectations
- Defined by other's whom God has put in our life

The natural mirror is defined by what you can be, or do, by your own strength and abilities.

The God-mirror is defined by what you can be, or do, in *His* strength and ability—through the Spirit who lives inside of you.

Transitioning into the God-mirror, through the renewing of the mind, *is not an option for believers!*

No discipleship happens outside of it!

So much of what I, and probably most of you, experienced if you had a Christian upbringing, was a message focused on taming the natural mirror and making it *good*. The result was *behavior modification (i.e.* compliant actions, with little heart satisfaction). Yet, there *is* a more excellent way!

Two Parts to the God-Mirror

To move into the reality of your God-mirror, you must understand both phases of the mirror. The first one is *who you are in Christ*, and the second is *who Christ is in you*. I process these two aspects differently.

Phase One: Who You Are in Christ

What we have, and who we are in Christ is the same for every believer. In Christ we all are:
- Justified
- Loved
- A new creation in Christ Jesus
- Forgiven
- Empowered
- A partaker of His promises
- A partaker of the divine nature
- Reconciled
- Crucified with Christ
- Blessed with all spiritual blessings
- Given all things that pertain to life and godliness
- Brought near by the blood of Christ
- Delivered from the power of darkness
- And much more!

All of us share these same blessings, and *our heritage as believers is to walk in the privileges of the finished work of Christ.*

Phase Two: Who Christ is in You

Together we all have the blessings listed above, but who Christ is in you/me/us makes us all different—unique. Finding your God-mirror, and the triumph therein, is a journey of discovering both who you are in Christ and who Christ is in you.

Ruthie and I are different. Who Christ is in Ruthie, manifests differently than who Christ is in me. Romans 12 and 1 Corinthians 12, relate the plan for our diversity—how we all, though different from each other, fit together to make the complete body of Christ, which refers back to the previous chapters on metrons.

Helping people discover who Christ is in them, and who they are in Christ, is the essence of discipleship. It is largely what church is all about. It is the focus of maturing in Christ. It is what sets God's people apart from those without Him.[3]

But there is a problem!

The problem with discovering the God-mirror is that *nobody can fully discover the God-mirror by themselves.* Neither you, nor I, were given the wisdom to find our glorious new creation in Christ Jesus by ourselves.

So then, what do we do?

In the next two chapters, I want to take you to another level that unveils the spirit and power of a kingdom culture.

---

[3] Several years ago, I decided to write a story that illustrated what I believed to be one of the most important lessons in the life-building process. I ended up with a short fable called, *You've Been Tweeked!* It is a story that reveals the battle surrounding one's journey toward the God-mirror—because what you think about yourself will be your greatest challenge on this journey. For more information, please visit my online store at: https://www.brucelengeman.com/store.

THE GOD-MIRROR
Questions

1. How do you process the statement: "Your greatest challenge in life is what you think about yourself"?

2. Have you falsely defined yourself by the influence of any of the following: parents, peers, circumstances, society, authorities? Renounce each false definition you may have agreed with. Ask others to pray with you as you do this.

3. Do you know that you are celebrated by God? If not, what do you think has kept you from accepting this truth?"

23

CALLING TO LIFE

A beautiful thing never gives so much pain as does failing to hear and see it.

—Michelangelo

So, if no one can discover the God-mirror by themselves, where do we go from here? What brings the body together is that *God has given each of us the privilege of calling each other to life.* Calling each other to life is the essence of *church life.* It is supported by the dozens of "one another's" in the Bible, which define all the ways we call each other to life—to our own God-mirror. The truth of the little poem I wrote that opened this section is that *I need you to reveal to me my potential in Christ,* and I will never get there without you—and you need me in the same way.

Therefore, in the kingdom culture, you must be engaged to see, to give, and to walk alongside of me, and I with you—to awaken what is asleep or revive what is dormant within. And lest you casually passed by the opening quote by Michelangelo, here it is again: "*A beautiful thing never gives so much pain as does failing to hear and see it.*"

Calling to life *means*:
- Affirming the potential of others.
- Showing them the image you see in *their* God-mirror.
- Helping others see what is hindering them from being everything they were designed to be.
- Encouraging others in their journey through life.
- Listening to God for others, and then sharing with them His love.
- Helping others see that their God-mirror is vastly more powerful than their natural mirror.

Another Michelangelo Quote and the God-Mirror

One of the best quotes ever about the God-mirror—in the history of the world, by anybody on this planet, or on any other planet—is another quote by Michelangelo. There are many different variations of this quote, but essentially it says, "When asked how he created such glorious sculptures, Michelangelo responded, 'I see the perfect, final sculpture inside the piece of marble and then I simply remove what doesn't belong.'" Another variation: "I saw the angel in the marble, and carved until I set him free."

(Pause to ruminate.)

Does this quote not characterize the *gusto* of relationships? In order to exist in the kingdom culture, each of us must have the same ability as Michelangelo—we must be able to see the glory in others, their potential, the finished product, and then help each other chip away at what does not belong.

Isn't this the way God walks with us? He always sees that finished product. David cried out in the Psalms in several places, "Oh God, if you would mark iniquities, who can stand!"

Along the way, I have had incredible friends, and brief acquaintances, who have called me to life. They saw the angel within and carved until I came free. They loved me when I was just a *chunk of junk*, and helped me remove what didn't belong, until my "angel" appeared. This is what *calling to life* is all about...*and this is the heart of the kingdom culture.*

Inmates and the Image of God

Back around 1995, a program was designed by the local prison chaplain to train twelve prison inmates. For twelve weeks, every evening, the prisoners came to class to be discipled and taught. There were five teachers, one for each evening. My day was Monday. I don't remember my topic.

The first day in class they were normal prison guys, peeing to mark their territory, letting me know they were in charge, and that I, probably, had nothing to offer them. How funny. They were in orange uniforms behind walls of steel, while I was living in freedom, yet they still wanted me to bow to their intimidation. I didn't. In fact, I did the opposite. I was not threatened in the least by their macho bravado or the distance they had put between themselves and me. I knew something—that every one of those men was created in the image of God, and whether or not they knew it, they all had a God-mirror—an angel within. My job was *not* to address their outward facade, but to speak life to their God mirror—to begin chiseling away what didn't belong.

By week three, they were lining up after class just to shake my hand, to express appreciation, or to confide in me the pains of their heart. By the end of the twelve weeks, we were tight friends, and most of them were learning to walk daily in their God-mirror.

Below are a few simple glimpses of calling others to life:

Bruce Freaks Ruthie Out without Giving Mercy

In 1987, I was hired as a counselor, speaker, and writer, for a well-established ministry. On my first-day orientation, John, the director, informed me that Ruthie and I would be teaching the *Positive*

Parenting seminar. When I got home, I was so excited! I told Ruthie the great news—which was *NOT* good news to her.

"*You* are teaching the seminar, right?"

"No, Hon, *we* are!"

"No, *you* are! I am not a teacher, *you* are."

"Sorry, it's a package deal, so get used to it—you and me—not me!"

"How could you do this to me?"

"I love you!"

The day came for the first *Positive Parenting* seminar. Ruthie was so stressed she had a fever, but she taught well. Soon Ruthie became comfortable with teaching that seminar, but nothing else. My task of calling Ruthie to life in the arena of public speaking was pure *tough love*. I knew she had it in her, and she got no pity from me. Now, Ruthie speaks confidently and with an anointing, by my side, at conferences for women, in small groups, and at most of our training seminars. I can even spontaneously call her up front while I am speaking and ask her to teach something that might be relevant. She is very grateful that I pursued her God-mirror and chipped away the insecurity that didn't belong.

One Life-Giving Comment Changes a Life

In *The Eight Habit*, author Steven R. Covey shares a great story:

> While on an international trip many years ago, I remember being introduced to a young man about eighteen-years-old. He had had some great challenges in his youth, including drug and alcohol abuse. Though he was turning his life around, as the two of us visited alone, I could tell that he was struggling for a sense of direction and doubted himself. I also discerned that he was a special young man, full of greatness and real potential. It beamed from his

countenance and spirit. Before we parted, I looked him right in the eye and told him that I believed he would be a person of great influence in the world throughout his life, and that he had unusual gifts and potential.

Almost twenty years later, he has become one of the most promising, able young men I know. He has a beautiful family and is a professional of real accomplishment. A friend of mine was recently visiting with him. During their conversation, this young man spontaneously recounted the experience I described above. Of it, he said, "You have no idea how that one hour impacted my life. I was told I was someone with potential that far surpassed what I had ever imagined. That thought caught hold inside me. It has made all the difference in the world."[4]

Chester the Shy Guy

Whenever we stopped for a meal in the small restaurant, Chester was always behind the counter. He was in his late thirties and never smiled or talked. He cooked and cleaned. Sometimes, he refilled our coffee, but he never connected on a personal level. I began chipping away at Chester's protective walls by being friendly and asking questions, trying to get to know him. Before long, Chester was talking blue streaks to us when we came in. We were able to encourage him, and he smiled when he talked to us. I often wondered if anybody else ever tried to break into Chester's heart—maybe so—but probably not many.

Tony Tells About Teddy

One of my favorite stories of calling to life is told by Tony Campolo about Teddy Stoddard. Rereading it still brings tears to my eyes. I'm not going to include it here for space reasons, but I encourage

---

[4] Stephen R Covey, *The 8th Habit: From Effectiveness to Greatness* (London: Simon & Schuster, 2006), 73.

you go to http://www.ccemmaus.com/teddy.html to read the full story.

Dry Bones and Calling to Life

You can do all the right things to create a life-giving culture, but without calling to life, you may be left with measly, old dry bones. What makes dry bones come alive is being in an environment where they are being called to life by those who can see the angel within every person. Nothing defines the essence of true church more than *calling to life*. May God put His presence in your culture to create an environment where everyone is committed to helping everyone else be their best!

"I saw an angel
in the marble
then carved until
I set him free"
a quote by
Michaelangelo
but those same
eyes
I want
for me

lo, we all are
rough, unformed,
we all are
undefined,
but love sees
something deeper
where commonly
we're blind

oh to have the eyes
to see
what eludes the
average man
oh to help
a piece of rock
embrace a finer,
more glorious
plan

for they
cannot themselves
perceive
the angel locked

inside
oft the hope
of something great
has
faded,
disappeared,
or died

let me use a chisel
Lord,
where You created
more,
grace me,
as an artist
to reveal
an angel's core

let me see in others
the majesty
hidden away
give me Lord
the skill to free
their masterpiece
to display

"I saw an angel
in the marble
then carved until
I set him free"
oh, what eyes
what piercing eyes,
but those are eyes
I want
for me

CALLING TO LIFE
Questions

1. When asked how he created such glorious sculptures, Michelangelo responded, "I see the perfect, final sculpture inside the piece of marble and then I simply remove what doesn't belong." How does this amazing answer process in your heart?

2. How can you do, in real life, what Michelangelo did with marble, with regards to the people you live and work with?

3. How can you become more conscious to practice more words of encouragement when speaking to others?

24

HEART

Trevor was asked to come to a meeting with the director of the large, nonprofit organization he worked for. The meeting was significant because a year ago, the director decided to make a shift in the organization. Trevor had worked hard in his position for over five years and had done exceptionally well. Also, he had been instrumental in transforming a culture that had previously been hurting and negative, to one that was positive and thriving.

At the time this new change occurred, the director came to Trevor with a plan for a major change, which he had learned from a new book he read. Trevor knew the plan would not work, but his several appeals fell on deaf ears. Heartbroken, Trevor was placed at the mercy of the new initiative—a move that stripped him of his primary influence in the organization. Not only was Trevor wounded in the process, but the people working in the department that Trevor oversaw were wounded also. Trevor stayed on and worked with the new initiative as diligently as possible, but his effectiveness was gone.

After a season, Trevor, a bit suspicious, was asked to come to a meeting with the director in his office, but he sensed beforehand that pleading his cause would be to no avail. At the meeting, the director began, with a statement to Trevor, admitting that he had taken a "formula" and bypassed Trevor's heart and the heart of his department. He went on to confess that he did this in order to initiate a more efficient protocol, but that the way he accomplished his purpose was unacceptable.

Trevor was then given permission to share how the initiative had affected him. He told the director that he felt as if he and the people under him were treated as *machines* instead of a group of living, breathing people who cared. The meeting ended on a positive note, and it created a platform for healing.

Heart.

As much as we teach and preach the gospel, too often, we miss the point—or said another way, we miss the *heart*. The older I get and the longer I labor in the kingdom, the more I learn the importance of always going to the heart, and the more I learn how much God's people have tried to function without it—in church, in business, in marriage, with kids, with friends, with coworkers, in evangelism, in teaching, and in discipleship.

Heart—we desperately need it!

Heart is about the real reason.

Heart is about the core motive.

Heart is about the real you.

Heart is about relationship over process.

Heart is about what you feel and what you think.

Heart is about your story.

Heart is about your journey.

Heart is about suffering together.

Heart is about *love*.

I have seen many ministry leaders, I have counseled many marriages, and I have advised many business executives who have tried to exist without supporting the hearts of those they work with side-by-side. I have witnessed and been a member of churches that put the organization above the organism. I have also seen many leaders die to leading, because, in their endeavors to succeed and do well, there was nobody to hold their heart, to simply be a friend, to care, or to walk alongside of them.

Bandanas & Harleys—The Night Whiskey Drinkers Cried

For over a decade, a significant part of my ministry involved ministering to very conservative religious groups—Amish, Mennonite, Brethren, etc. I was never a part of a conservative church like that, but God opened door after door, and this ministry focus worked well for me, even though I never filled out an application to God asking for it.

One day, I got a call from a pastor who was given my name as a recommendation. He invited me to speak at a men's retreat. It wasn't a big gig, but I felt like God wanted me to accept his invitation. The retreat was with a group of guys from an environment I am not accustomed to or active in. They were definitely *not* conservative.

Friday evening of the retreat, I met the group in a parking lot where we would follow each other to the remote cabin. When I arrived at the lot, I panicked. These guys had rusted trucks, bandanas (the kind motorcycle gangsters wear), many tattoos (yep!), and some were getting in a quick smoke before leaving. Suddenly, I realized how out of place I was. I had no problem with the tattoos, the smokes, or the red-neck bumper stickers, but I feared that I had forgotten how to relate to those being saved out of the world and not out of religion. While the people I had ministered to for a decade were getting free of rules, dress codes, churchianity, and other religious baggage, these guys had been whiskey drinkers, womanizers, even some enjoyed rap music—yep! One guy in the parking lot told me his "old lady" was mad at him for coming and leaving her with the kids. "Your wife?" I asked. "No, my old lady!" he responded.

Now, don't wrongly profile me—I've got some red-neck blood in my own bones. Sometimes at my church, I preach in my bare feet. I once rode a go-cart at Hershey Park—a fast one! I even had a tattoo of my own—granted, it was from a pack of Bazooka Bubble Gum. Nevertheless, a tattoo is a tattoo, right? Until the zipper broke, I even wore a black leather jacket, and before I was saved I smoked *Cool Menthols*—not exactly a nerd smoke. I'm not intentionally trying to impress you—though, I probably did—I'm just saying, it wasn't what these guys were doing that jolted me, it was the fear that I didn't know how to minister to them anymore.

If I remember correctly, we got to the cabin somewhere near *Mad Grizzly Forge Valley Ravine*. Rustic is generous there. We were all to sleep in the giant, open upstairs. The decor was *contemporary prison cell*. I picked the bed farthest from any other bed, by the wall, hoping the ones who forgot to bring their C-PAP anti-snore machine wouldn't bunk beside me. When it was time to start the meeting, we went to the auditorium where there were a bunch of tree stumps surrounding a campfire. (Did I mention that they all brought their guns along?) They sang a few choruses (such as, "*House of the Rising Sun*") and then Pastor Matthew introduced me. He apologized there was no speaker's podium. He asked me if I was okay with that. I paused, for an uncomfortable length of time and then, responded (really, this part is true), "Actually, I don't even know what I'm speaking on!" And I was serious!

Right then and there, I scrapped my notes in favor of *going to their hearts*.

Without notes, I began speaking to their hearts, teaching these men the importance of going to the heart with their wives, children, and in the church. Connecting to hearts, I told them, is not a feminine thing. It is masculine, and the world needs men who know how to release their own heart and hear the hearts of others.

The next morning, I continued with the same message. Before I was finished, half these rugged, tough guys, who still listen to *The Rolling Stones'* songs, had tears in their eyes. Then, around the campfire, they went to the heart, one by one, sharing pain, disappointment, readiness to change, and commitments to begin caring in a new way—Pastor Matthew, too! They told their stories—their life stories, and when they did, we all listened, and we all cared.

I left that weekend feeling more fulfilled than if I had been the keynote speaker for a conference of thousands at a conference center in Hawaii. The reason why? *We went to the heart.*

One of the guys who got the most wrecked that weekend, in a good way, was the one whose *old lady* was angry. Not too long after the retreat, they were married.

Uncovering the God-mirror in others, by calling them to life, will only happen when we are committed to going heart-to-heart, instead of head-to-head. Most of the church, as I have known it, has been quite good—and *in*effective—at going head-to-head. We have ineffectively gone head-to-head in evangelism, instead of heart-to-heart. We have tried to shepherd the sheep only with doctrine, theology and *shoulds,* and we have produced a massive culture of spiritual orphans. We have been leaders, instead of fathers and mothers. Many church people today are *taught-out,* and *love-starved.*

In Acts 13:22, David is called *a man after God's heart.* If you study the life of David, you'll see how imperfect he was. He made lots of mistakes, and some of those mistakes were costly to him and to his nation. But despite David's imperfections, he maintained his favor with God as a man after God's heart.

Most violations *to* a healthy culture and most divisions *in* a healthy culture, come because somewhere along the line, somebody failed to hear someone else's heart.

This past Sunday, Ruthie and I preached at our church on the topic of marriage. It was the 39th anniversary of my having asked Ruthie to marry me. We were able to proclaim the wonderfulness of marriage and how every single year was better than the last. If I could list the keys to our success in marriage, I would put at the top of the list that we learned to relate to each other heart-to-heart. It was not easy. It took work—through many disagreements, mistakes, and personality changes. But we were committed to the process, and it worked—and still works.

Hey, won't you take a look at me
tell me, friend,
tell me what you see
A man of spirit,
full of life and free,
my act together
don't you agree?

but take a little closer look
turn the cover of my book
inside unveils a heart of pain
read a page
and I'll explain

Joking on the surface
crying deep inside
hiding broken places
where once hope occupied
each and every second
struggling to survive
every moment feeling dead
pretending I'm alive

It's easy to impress you
when you're not looking deep
down below my cool charade
and see the tears I weep

don't you see
I'm holding
a mask up to my face
watch my dance and see
the awesome style
and the grace

the Great Pretender
once again
I wish that every now and then
a caring soul would not be fooled
and hold my heart
that's growing
cold.

help me live, yes
help me cope
with words that heal
my heart with hope
navigate to
the real, true me
then please
please
revive
my destiny.

HEART
Questions

1. "Going to the heart" is a vital essential to maintaining a kingdom culture. What are practical ways you can be a vital part of creating "heart" in your culture?

2. Discuss the statement on page 189: "Most violations *to* a healthy culture and most divisions *in* a healthy culture came, because somewhere along the line, somebody failed to hear someone else's heart."

3. David is called a man after God's heart. Using King David as a role model, why is *going to the heart* not considered weak or predominantly *feminine?*

25

The Virtue of Listening

You can make more friends in two months by becoming interested in other people than you can in two years by trying to get other people interested in you.
—Dale Carnegie

Number One of Two Incidents

Recently, I ran into a man whom Ruthie and I are very close to. He grabbed me and gave me a hug. He is an influential man and has thanked me countless times for believing in him and walking him through significant changes in his life. But today was bitter-sweet. He said, "I called my dad yesterday, simply because I needed him to ask me how things were going in my life. But, like usual, he kept on talking about all sorts of little things about himself and never asked me how things were going with me." My friend got off the phone discouraged and disappointed. His point in telling me this was to thank me for stepping in as a father figure when his father didn't. This younger man's affirmation of me was priceless—humbling. So many great things are happening in this man's life. Unfortunately, the person he wants to care about him the most, doesn't seem to, and the one he wants to rejoice with him the most, won't.

I tell this episode because, more and more, our society—even in the "Christian" culture—seems self-centered, and nowhere is it more evident than in what we say in conversation with people—and what we don't say.

Ruthie and I continue to be stunned by how so many good people and leaders we meet with, are into their own agendas—their own opinions and ideas. They give testimony of themselves—even if it seems to be in the name of God and goodness. The problem is that people often don't even think to say, *"But how are things going with you?"*

...and then listen to the answer.

Incident Number Two

The day after incident one, above, Ruthie had breakfast with a close friend. She came home thrilled to be with her. She told me that her friend was going through a lot, and so most of the conversation was about her friend. This was not painful to Ruthie and not the least bit negative. It wasn't out of place, because Ruthie was happy to listen to her friend, knowing that she is not in any way a self-focused person, but this was Ruthie's turn to be a listening ear. This friend is always a *giver* in relationships.

But no sooner had Ruthie told me this when an email came her way:

> Ruthie, I left our time together this morning feeling blessed that we could share a few hours together, and I do appreciate your interest in what's going on in my life and heart. However, afterward, I went, "What was I thinking?" I didn't even ask you about your experience in Haiti!! Or invited anything else on your heart you may have wanted to share with me (sad smile). So I just wanted to say, if you feel you have the time this week and desire

to share about that, please feel free to call me. If not, we can catch up with that another time. But I wanted you to know that I would sometime like to hear about "your heart in Haiti" and feel badly that I took up so much of the time to share about our situation...Boo. I know you won't hold it against me, but *I just wanted to say that I desire for our times together to be give and take, not just give for you and take for me.* I appreciate you and will join the "praying friends back home" as you venture out once more. Kingdom work! May God cheer your heart and supply you with strength for the journey.
-Cheri

Ruthie didn't need a reply from her friend, but that it came, affirmed the quality character and deep heart of the friendship she has with her. It also illustrates what this teaching is about—*getting out of your own self focus enough to value the hearts of others.*

The Truth That Helped Me the Most

How to Win Friends and Influence People by Dale Carnegie[5] is a timeless classic. Much of it is both simple and profound. I am just one of the countless multitudes who have been influenced by this book. I read just two random pages again last night and was re-influenced.

One of the chapters in Dale's book that helped me the most is titled, "Do This and You'll Be Welcome Anywhere." It is about being interested in others as a way of life. It is about listening to others— their stories, their endeavors, their heart. Life doesn't work when our goal is trying to get people interested in us: "Friends, real friends," Dale writes, "are not made that way." (I would love to copy and paste the whole chapter here. It's that incredible! I hope you read the book. Although Mr. Carnegie doesn't use all the same approaches and

---

[5] Dale Carnegie, *How to Win Friends and Influence People* (New York: New York, Simon and Schuster [c1964], 1937), 56.

terminology I do, his book is largely about kingdom culture.)

Unfortunately, a Dunce Hat for Many!

Ruthie and I were discussing our journey in finding mentors to walk alongside us during our ministry work. We reflected back over a couple of men we thought could walk with us through life, and we tried them out. But all they wanted to do was teach us. Mentorships such as this don't last long. You see, mentorship is more than just teaching, you must also take the time to listen to the other's journey. Fortunately, we *did* find that in some.

For several years, Ruthie and I were teachers at a parent-teen seminar. In one session, I would open by showing the audience a piece of paper folded and cut into a cone shape. Then I would ask the audience to tell me what it was. Of course, only *I* knew the answer. I got a variety of answers: ice cream cone, funnel, dunce hat, party hat, orange traffic cone, a cake-decorating icing cone, Hershey's kiss, unicorn horn, space craft, and cornucopia. I even heard it described as a megaphone. Then I gave the correct answer: an ear trumpet—a devise for listening—and I would proceed with my lesson on *Listening to Other's Hearts*.

Ruthie and I continue to be stunned by how many leaders we meet, or chat with, are only into their own agendas, their own opinions and ideas, and give testimony only of themselves—even if it seems to be in the name of God. Unfortunately, they don't think to show value, care, or interest to other's hearts and lives.

A Tale of Two Pastors

Lonnie and I came to town at the same time. We were both new pastors with similar doctrines and approaches, so we decided to chat over chow every now and then. The first time we chatted, I saw Lonnie's passion. He could crank out profound insights like the Hershey Chocolate Factory cranks out kisses. I excused his conversation-domination as excitement for God. The next time, my assistant came with me to chat and chow. He, too, noticed something about Lonnie: Hook a generator to that boy's tongue and we could've lit the whole city. To say we were overwhelmed was an understatement. This happened again and again, and then the last time. We soon realized, though Lonnie loved the Lord, he didn't care about much outside of hearing his own voice, and he was probably that way with his congregation, too. His agenda was to share his own thoughts and ideas—period.

The conversation went like this: Lonnie would share for ten minutes—suddenly a pause—I would quickly inject some of my own comments, attempting to dialogue with him, but his listening span was less than twenty seconds, then he would sabotage the dialogue and yank it back to his court. I would say the same phrases every time we got together: "*Uh huh, yeah, okay, yes, uh huh*," and when someone else talked, he would promptly interrupt.

The relationship didn't last long. Lonnie was indeed a teacher, but nobody enjoys being taught all the time!

If Lonnie was on the North Pole, Bill Nissen was on the South. When I moved to small-town Iowa, Grace, a woman I had never met, heard about Ruthie and me and visited our home. She told me (not *asked*) that she was taking me to Bill's church, about an hour away. Ruthie and I went with Grace. While standing in the back of the church, pre-service, Bill (a massive, good-looking, six foot nine monstrosity) saw me and introduced himself. He then asked what I did for a living. I told him, I am a teacher, counselor, writer, blah, blah, blah. He immediately asked me to join him for a chat-and-chow on Tuesday morning.

Oh right! I thought. *Good pastor—merchandise me from the beginning! Get me to go to his church and then use me to build his own agenda. Hey, Buddie, I've been around. I know the games, the strategies, the corrupt motives. But I'll go along with it and see what happens.*

"Sure, I'll meet you. What time and where?"

I met Bill at Perkins for breakfast. He paid my bill. He never talked to me about coming to his church—not that time. Never did. We became friends. I came back to his church every now and then, but not regularly. When I met with Bill, MY agenda was always his focus. He always listened. Yeah, he told some about his, but he always seemed more concerned about mine and all the other people who, in the next few years, met together with us. Bill had died to churchy games and personal-platform-building long before I had met him. It freed him to go the heart of those God put in his path. You couldn't give surface answers to Bill when he asked, *"How ya doin'?"* He would go deep and deeper, until he got the truth and then, he found some way to affirm or encourage you. It was hard to out-listen Bill.

Bill is a man of great authority. Somewhere along the way, however, he took some grief because he didn't go along with the main stream of what many Christians promote. He knew that God is all about the heart and about relationships. I don't live in Iowa any more. I don't talk to Bill much, but every time I do, I know he still cares. He is now, in addition to being a successful pastor, a successful businessman.

Time and again, Ruthie and I meet with mature believers and leaders, and we leave stunned at how much people can be into their own agenda. We don't judge, though we often sorrow, for when we point the finger, there are always three fingers pointing back at us. This is not to condemn us, but rather to remind us that most of the time, it is better to listen than to talk. As I mentioned earlier, I am constantly reminded of the quote by Theodore Roosevelt: *Nobody cares how much you know, until they know how much you care.*

Chronic Flap-Jaw Syndrome

Over-talking is a plague! Many people can talk a blue streak in conversation and never notice that they failed to create dialogue, failed to draw in the other with questions, or if they asked, they didn't listen to the full response. I have challenged Ruthie to avoid certain people simply because they will abuse her ear and are oblivious to their own motor-mouth. They hate to be interrupted, but they perpetually interrupt others.

People who understand a kingdom culture understand the art of listening. The *art of listening* is not a trivial or petty point to the subject of this book, but it is a major point. So much of the kingdom culture—calling to life, going to the heart, preferring others above yourself, and basic love—*all* surround this one crucial skill.

Over-talking is one of the most hard-to-see blind spots for people.

Ruthie often shares her own victory from *over-active-tongue* disease. Honestly, it didn't come easy. It was years into our marriage before we crossed this pain line. I never minded Ruthie's talking when Ruthie was talking to me, but I got to a point that I couldn't be passive any longer when she would dominate me in social settings and in counseling. When I would address it, Ruthie was often defensive, because she felt that I was shutting her down. She would then overreact and say, *"Well, then, I just won't talk."* We would get through it, and she would sincerely ask God for eyes to see. But honestly, it was a stronghold and a blind spot, which took many confrontations.

At times, she would ask me why I was so quiet when we were with friends. I would respond, *"Because you don't pause long enough for me to get a word in edgewise. You comment on what others say faster than a speeding bullet. You interrupt my thought process before I am finished."* Obviously, this did not make Ruthie feel like she does when she is eating coffee-mocha gelato. Nonetheless, she sought God on it. She asked me to continue to point out her blind spot to her and adopted a more low-profile posture, for a while, when we were with others.

As time went on, God went to the root in Ruthie's heart and pulled out lies that were driving her talkativeness. One was that she felt responsible for other's social enjoyment, as well as a few other lies. Suddenly, she began noticing other people who un-blessed others with the same verbal motor. She would ask, *"Was I that bad? God forbid!"*

Ruthie regularly thanks me for helping her overcome this habit now that she fully understands how listening works in a kingdom culture. In private, she often points out to others what they are doing when she sees them verbally shutting down their spouse or friends. She doesn't talk less than me, and at times, it is appropriate for her to talk much more than me. The key is, when we are together, we verbally dance with each other.

My Listening Issue

I, too, had a problem with listening. Although these were different from Ruthie's, I was no better than her. I still have a long way to go before I have mastered the art of listening, though it is always a major priority in my life to master it. My problem is that I am a processor. Often, when people were talking with me, I would *detach* to process what they were saying, without even knowing I had detached. I have worked hard to overcome this reaction and learn to fully concentrate on what people are saying to me without detaching. Much of this came from my reaction growing up, having nobody to listen to me and nobody ever pursuing my heart. It took Ruthie, many times, addressing this issue with me before I was able to catch it and stop the process of processing.

As I mentioned above, I first learned about the importance and power of listening several decades ago when I read *How to Win Friends and Influence People*. I have had several of my children read the book. I told all of them, at one point or another, if you want to be an influencer, you must prepare to always listen more than you talk. Listeners make the kingdom culture glisten, because, most of the time, *listeners are listeners because they esteem others more important than themselves as a habit.*

When you are enjoying relationship with another—your spouse, your friend, at a team meeting, in a group or social setting—ask questions that engage others to express their ideas, thoughts, feelings, opinions, observations, and then allow them to finish their thoughts, before jumping in with the million comments trying to bust out of your mind and through your tongue. Temperance and restraint are disciplines when it comes to the tongue.

James 3:3-9 is dedicated to bridling the tongue. Read a few verses from this chapter:

> Even so the tongue is a little member and boasts great things. See how great a forest a little fire kindles! And the tongue is a fire, a world of iniquity. The tongue is so set among our members that it defiles the whole body, and sets on fire the course of nature; and it is set on fire by hell. For every kind of beast and bird, of reptile and creature of the sea, is tamed and has been tamed by mankind. But no man can tame the tongue. It is an unruly evil, full of deadly poison. (James 3:5-8)

We understand through this passage that mastering the tongue is a characteristic of those who are mature.

Over-talking is a scourge in any kind of relationship.

Conclusion: Why Trying To Stop Over-Talking Won't Work!

Over-talking is a scourge in any kind of relationship, but *trying to stop over-talking won't solve the problem.* The problem will be solved on the heart level, when you make the choice to "esteem others more important than yourself" (Philippians 2:3). It will happen when you make a sincere choice to deny your own platform building and choose to care more about others, rather than yourself. May God give us all a fresh revelation of love. And if I can leave you with a challenge: After committing yourself to His fresh love, aim as much as possible, to speak 49 percent or less of the words in most of your conversations.

The more you esteem others more important, the more they will esteem you!

The Talker

We had a lot in common
this guy I met last week
"Hey, how about some breakfast
down at Rusty Creek?"

I'd great anticipation
for this rendezvous,
I get a bit excited
'bout meeting someone
new

At first we chatted small talk
Then he began to share
all sorts of things
about himself
(I sat silent
in my chair.)

I thought
he might be lonely
for a listening ear
but after fifty minutes
I hoped to
disappear.

This man
indeed
was gifted
(he subtly let me know)
he had some great opinions
(I know,
he told me so).

He never thought to ask me
"What's happening with you?"
He never paused to care
about my point of view.
Three times I interjected
something that I knew
to which he listened
intently
for a second
(maybe
two).

He wowed me with his stories,
impressed me with his wit
told me all his history
talked
and never quit.

His life was helping others,
but somehow he couldn't see
that in his selfish focus,
he disregarded me.

A man of great distinction
like no one else!
I bet
a man of many syllables,
I wish
I never met.

THE VIRTUE OF LISTENING
Questions

1. What do you think about Dale Carnegie's quote: "You can make more friends in two months by becoming interested in other people than you can in two years by trying to get other people interested in you"?

2. What do you think motivates people to dominate conversations?

3. Discuss this statement: "People who have healthy self-worth don't have to always be promoting their agendas, thoughts, ideas, and feelings in conversation with others, but are free to serve others, when appropriate, by a listening ear."

26

THREE VITAL HABITS THAT GIVE LIFE TO A KINGDOM CULTURE

Although what I'm about to share with you may seem simple or primitive, it is crucial to understanding the spirit of the kingdom culture. Please do not skip over these three vital, but often neglected, habits that give life to a *kingdom culture*.

One: The Habit of Gratitude

While the habit of gratitude is basic, it is one of the most important concepts in this book. Without appreciation and gratitude, the kingdom culture will *flop*. If you lead an organization, ask yourself how often or how well you and your team express value and appreciation to those who make the organization work.

Yesterday, Ruthie and I had the wonderful privilege of having some one-on-one time with the author of some of my favorite books, Bruce Main. The first book I read of his was, *Why Jesus Crossed the Road*. In it, Main injected the heart of God into my spirit like few books ever have or probably ever will.

Bruce Main founded *Urban Promise,* a ministry in the city of Camden, NJ. Unfortunately, Camden is ranked as one of the most dangerous cities in the US, with crime rates massively higher than other cities. *Urban Promise* hosts hundreds of volunteers and interns each year. Young adults come from all over the country to give a portion of their life, sacrificing career pursuits and financial gain, to give to the children of Camden.

When we arrived at *Urban Promise* headquarters, I introduced myself to Bruce Main as *The Main Bruce,* to which I got no response. This was probably an old, overused, dead humor line to him. Nonetheless, I laughed inside myself at my own joke. Then we sat in Main's office, while he answered our questions and told us stories tucked away in the archives of the ministry.

After our chat-time, Bruce took us around the school and explained that day was the first of their seven-week Bible camp. They were hosting Bible camp in nine locations around Camden. Hundreds of young people were a part of the camp. Our tour was interrupted several times because Bruce could hardly walk by someone without extending a warm greeting and telling Ruthie and me, in front of them, what they do and how well they do it.

Ruthie and I chatted with interns, staff, and witnessed the success of the ministry. One such man was teaching young children. He had come up through the program. The ministry assisted him in getting his college degree, and now he was in the *giving* seat. Several of his family members are in prison.

I sensed something real, as I listened and questioned a few of the staff. I sensed that Urban Promise is a kingdom culture that practices the habit of *gratitude.* I am not into fluffy flattery, but nothing generates life in a kingdom culture more than gratitude. The definition of gratitude is *the quality of being thankful; readiness to show appreciation for and to return kindness.*

Practice the habit of *lavish* gratitude in your culture. Again, I am not talking about cheap, formal fluff—but honest affirmation of others who are contributing to your culture, from your children and wife at home, to your boss—give honor and gratitude where it is due.

Two: The Habit of Having Fun

Ruthie and I laugh a lot. I won't even begin to tell you some of our inside jokes. We laugh at our elder's meetings at church. We laugh in the church services. I try to make my seminars a blast, even though I have the tendency to be inconceivably bizarre. My children complain about my dumb jokes, to which I always reply, *"Would you rather I be boring?"* You may be surprised to learn they often reply with a hearty, *"Yes!"*

Many years ago, I was the pastor of a church I planted. Our elder's meetings were 10 percent business and 90 percent fun. Yes, I'm exaggerating, but you get the point. A few years into the church, I developed a relationship with another pastor of a church very similar to ours. He asked me at one point if our two leadership teams could meet together so my group could teach his group how to have fun. He told me his team never had fun.

We met together and had a blast. I had no idea that ten years later I would be the pastor of that very same church. And guess what? We *do* have fun!

Fun is vital in a healthy culture—not just fun in what we say, but fun in what we do. Schedule fun trips, play games, read Chuck Norris jokes, watch a movie, play a kosher joke on someone, chill, loosen up, laugh. 'Nuff said!

Three: The Habit of Cheerleading

At church, when we do our leadership internship, we invite married couples into the group. Every new addition to our group, at some point in the year, shares their leadership journey. After sharing their leadership history, we all gather around the one who shared and call him or her to life, as we listen to the Holy Spirit.

Susan and Darrell give a unique flare to our team. When it was Susan's turn to share her story, she told about being a cheerleader in high school and how cheerleading exemplifies who she is—"I love the *rah-rah* of life. I love passion and enthusiasm, encouraging people, and getting excited about the things of God!"

Every group needs cheerleaders. Not everybody has to be a *Susan,* but a team without the drive of passion and enthusiasm is like roller-skating on Myrtle Beach. Enthusiasm keeps things moving forward. Passion keeps the important things at the top of the list.

As leaders, we have the privilege of generating enthusiasm in our team. Boring meetings are often just on the left side of pond scum.

According to the Internet, as of today, there are 4,376 ways to generate enthusiasm and passion in your team. If you can't come up with any on your own, I am concerned for you. I challenge you and your team to come up with at least twenty-two of the 4,376 ways to make your team exciting.

Gratitude, fun, and passion—essentials for your kingdom culture. Don't just say, *"That's nice!"*

Live it,

Facilitate it,

Do something about it.

Enjoy it!

Three Vital Habits That Give Life to a Kingdom Culture
Questions

1. Discuss the importance of gratitude in your culture.

2. Discuss the importance of having fun in your culture

3. Discuss the importance of cheerleading—celebrating others—in your culture.

27

Transition in a Kingdom Culture

This chapter wasn't in my original outline, but the more I pondered it, the more I realized it may be an essential inclusion to complement what has already been said up to this point. Here's why:

Transition can be one of the most challenging dynamics to a kingdom culture.

I've heard it. I've said it—"I'm now in transition."

My View on Transition Has Changed

I once heard a preacher say he had *the ministry of transition*.

I don't use the term *transition* the same way as I did in the past. I used to view my spiritual journey as pretty peaceful, with *every-now-and-then* seasons of transition. Now, I view my journey as *transition with seasons of quiet rest from continuous change*. As believers, we need to *always* be growing. And if we are growing, we must be actively *transitioning* to meet the growth.

To me, the honest truth is that, generally, all change demands transitioning—*adapting to accommodate the change*. But changing, without transitioning, produces stress. If you are at A, and you need to go to D, transitioning means you must go through B and C. Doing this demands *the big three*: maturity, strong character, and godliness.

Realizing this necessary transition, going to D through B and C, was significantly helpful to me. Perhaps it will be helpful to you, also, to accept the fact that transition *is* constant. *If we are always growing, we are always transitioning.* Accepting this helped me accept that I am not a bizarre creature. I am a normal, constantly-changing human who has the privilege of managing continual transition in various arenas of life.

But What about the Seasons of Rest?

There are times when growth and change slow down. I have had such seasons. Sometimes, they feel as if God disappears or as if His anointing is gone. But it is during those times that we get a rest from transitioning and change, even a rest from growth as we have known it. I believe these seasons are designed by God to strengthen our faith and to help us dig deeper roots.

During those times of rest, we may think we have become complacent. During these periods, instead of "a day is with the Lord as a thousand years," it seems as if "a thousand years is as a day." Instead of God numbering the hairs of our head, we find ourselves in his historical plan—which transcends thousands of years—and our years are just Nano-seconds of time in that process. We wonder if He even sees us.

We learn in these seasons (of same-ol'-same-ol') to trust Him by faith, not by sight—not seeing or aware of all He is doing, not feeling all He is changing, and sensing little to nothing in the spirit. In these times, we develop contentment with what we have and are, instead of constantly striving for more. We learn to better use what we already know, instead of moving on to something new (without nurturing what we once learned).

Earlier in my life as a believer, I went through a dry time—at least it was in my mind. During that season the Bible didn't come alive. Profound revelation seemed non-existent. I wondered if something was wrong with me. That season lasted for months. I was concerned. Little did I know that my Father was teaching me to trust that He was every bit as present with me when I didn't feel Him as when I did. At the national Washington for Jesus Crusade of the late eighties, while sitting, listening to Winkie Pratney and Dawson McAllister, the dull cloud suddenly lifted—the passion returned, the Word came alive again, and I was stronger in faith than before this testing.

What I just described about seasons of dryness (where not much seems to happen), can be true of any church, business, or even a marriage. We can fight these seasons and try to hype things up, or be at rest in faith, knowing that droughts often cause plants to grow deeper roots for survival in coming days, and the fruit is more luscious.

What Got You Here, Won't Get You There!

You won't be around me very long before you hear me say, *"What got you here, won't get you there!"* whether it be in counseling, while consulting, to my kids, or preaching a sermon. I borrowed the term from Marshall Goldsmith in his book, *What Got You Here, Won't Get Your There.*[6]

I address quite a few applications with this phrase, but the application I want to emphasize here is this: The habits, practices, behaviors, principles, and strategies that were a part of getting you from where you were, to where you are now, are not necessarily what will get you from where you are now, to where you want or need to go.

This may apply to you personally, to your marriage, or to your organization. Simply stated, *we must transition. Same-ol'-same-ol'* philosophy may send you down the wrong path. Your initial vision was great back then—but *is it still your vision?* The way you communicated

---

6 Marshall Goldsmith and Mark Reiter, *What Got You Here Won't Get Your There: How Successful People Become Even More Successful!* (New York, NY: Hyperion, 2007).

worked—back at the beginning—but is it working now? Are your policies a fit for where you are? Do you need fresh ones?

Team Transition

The best way to keep transitioning is to have regular, scheduled times to get away with your team, even if your team means just you and your wife, to strategize how to bring freshness to your relationship. Tap into the intelligence and creativity of your team, and move forward with gusto!

And more than anything, transition demands lots of quality communication! The only way teams transition together, and stay on the same page, is by wrestling through the changes on the back of healthy communication. This is so important, especially when it means changing your policies, your traditions, your habits, your structures. Grow, but grow strong. Change, but change with the wind to your back, joining arms together as a team and letting God open the way in front of you.

Transition In A Kingdom Culture
Questions

1. Why is *transition* one of the most challenging dynamics to a kingdom culture?

2. Describe different levels of transition and change within a culture. How can you respond to each level?

3. One of my favorite statements is: *"What got you here, won't get you there!"* What does this mean to you, and how can you apply it to your culture?

28

IN THE BEGINNING

I began this book the same way I am ending it: *In the Beginning*. As I sit here on the floor, going through a ton of notes, articles, and books that I've collected over the years, I am slightly overwhelmed. In perusing these resources I came upon multitudes of nifty quotes and profound insights that needed to be included in this book. But, alas, does anyone want to read a two-thousand page book on the kingdom culture?

No.

So I piled up the extra resources and proclaimed a hearty, "Enough!" over my manuscript, knowing that, although incomplete, it *is* complete.

But why did I name this chapter "*In the Beginning?*" The answer is that I suspect this book may be a new beginning for you in your work and relationships. In some ways now having read this book, the real work begins—learning the kingdom culture—living the kingdom culture.

Perhaps someday I will write more on the topics discussed in this book. But, for now, I bless you in your journey, and I look forward to hearing how the concepts in this book may have altered your life.

In the beginning
means today
for each moment
I can say
that as I walk
my way
my mistakes
I need never
replay
and now
within my heart
is a brand new
pristine
start

a new beginning
yes,
with a chance
for more success,
a new chance
to dispossess
the villains
that oppress
and replace them
with the new
the fresh
the good
the true,
and this
I now pursue
knowing God...

will see me
through.

The Beginning!

In the Beginning
Questions

1. Having read the book, come up with ten ways to generate *life* in your culture.

2. Where do you and your team go from here in order to strengthen you kingdom culture?

3. What other topics would you have included in this book that seem important to you? Feel free to contact me via www.brucelengeman.com/form/contact-bruce and let me know.

About the Author

For over four decades Bruce has been in the life-building arena, helping others grow their lives, their ministries, their businesses--all for the glory of God. He and his wife, Ruthie, often team-teach the various seminars and training events they do, at churches, businesses, conferences--both in the US and internationally. In addition to teaching, Bruce is active as a consultant and personal mentor. Bruce says that his best application is leadership development: leading the leader, training the trainer, and counseling the counselor. He and Ruthie have nine children and sixteen grandchildren--and counting!

Bruce, and Bruce and Ruthie, are available for speaking engagements, consulting, including online consulting, Visit his website for more information.

Seminars, Conferences & Workshops

Bruce and Ruthie Lengeman are available to speak at your event or meeting. Contact them at info@BruceLengeman.com. Below are some of their seminar and workshop topics:

Marriage and Family

After over 35 years of marriage, Bruce and Ruthie claim their love for each other still gets stronger every day. They believe God wants every married couple to experience growing romance and vitality in their relationship. Bruce and Ruthie also believe many Christians are ready to go beyond the same basic stuff taught at many marriage seminars.

Bruce and Ruthie offer several different seminars for married couples including:

- Intimacy and Sexuality in Marriage
- Bountiful Union—for couples desiring to be fruitful in God's Kingdom—together!
- We're In This Together—A seminar designed to equip couples to experience a lifelong romance
- Productive Partnership for Leaders—Grow a thriving marriage in the midst of the pressures of leading others

Women

Ruthie is an amazing motivational speaker who loves helping women to be all they can be. She speaks on a variety of topics, but one of her favorite topics is *The Dangerous Woman*. Here Ruthie tells her testimonial of how God delivered her from what she calls *okayness*—when women stuff pain, dreams and desires and become *okay* with inner wounds or unfulfilled places in life and marriage. She challenges women to be the powerful person God designed them to be.

Business

One of Bruce's greatest passions is strengthening businesses and business people. Bruce was active for over a decade in business consulting and speaking at business-related events. Bruce is available for consultation in your organization or to speak at organizational conferences and training events.

Search for Bruce Lengeman on YouTube or Vimeo to watch video teachings of Bruce and Ruthie.

Audio teachings and a variety of written articles are available at www.BruceLengeman.com.

Stay up-to-date and be encouraged.
Follow Bruce on Twitter and Facebook.

Additional Resouces

Beyond Purity Seminar for Men on DVD or CD

Men cry, *"I know it's wrong, but why can't I stop?"*

Host your own Beyond Purity Seminar for Men, using Bruce Lengeman's 11-session course deigned to transform men at the root. Sessions are broken down into shorter teaching segments to help facilitate those who may use this resource at weekly gatherings for men. Discussion guides are available.

In this seminar created for groups or individuals, men will learn a healthy view of sexuality and how to destroy the power of lust at the root. Bruce also expands on major root issues that drive immorality: the father wound, the mother wound, rejection, low self-esteem, shame, male passiveness, sexual abuse and other male-related issues. Men will learn how to close immoral doors that they opened that have paved the way for Satan to plant strongholds in their hearts.

Order at www.BruceLengeman.com

To Kill a Lion and Companion Workbook

Men cry, *"I know it's wrong, but why can't I stop?"*

This is a common cry throughout our culture from Christian men who are seeking to find freedom from the nagging grip of sexual lust. In *To Kill a Lion*, Bruce Lengeman takes men beyond behavior modification and answers the question: "But what's driving the drive?" Some approaches to sexual purity adequately tell men, "It's bad! Don't do it!" but don't give men real solutions. To Kill a Lion is about destroying sexual roots. It is about who a man is, not just what he does.

In *To Kill A Lion*, you'll discover:

- How to be pure without being less sexual
- How to close sexual doors to Satan that you opened at some point
- How a man's sexuality is connected to almost everything in his life
- How to trace your sexual issues back to emotional issues
- How sexual freedom in your heart will bring new sexual vitality to your marriage
- How you can get to the place where you want sexual purity more than you want immorality

To Kill a Lion **Workbook Edition** features methods for effectively starting a group, as well as provoking questions for group discussion. This tool can also be used solely for personal growth. It will guide readers of To Kill a Lion to delve deeper into the roots of their sexual issues. It delivers practical application, which will enable men to obtain a deeper understanding of the underlying problems, leading them to sexual freedom and lifelong

You've Been Tweeked!

You've Been Tweeked! exposes the subtle battle inside every mind that determines why some people succeed and others fail. It uncovers the incredible secrets behind all successful self-improvement strategies that will unlock your doorway to destiny.

One businessman said, *"This is one of the ten best books I've ever read! It's the secret of overcoming everything!"*

Another reader commented, *"Enlightening…explaining controlling mechanisms in my own mind that I never even thought of before."*

"Why me?" people cry out.

"Why can't I get ahead?"

"Why can't I fix my marriage?"

"Why can't I change my behavior?"

You've Been Tweeked! will challenge the business person, the parent, the teacher, the teenager, and others. If you are depressed, addicted, confused, not living to your full potential, or struggling with failure, you will not only benefit from *You've Been Tweeked!*, but you will pass it on to a friend. An average reader can read this book in an afternoon.

You've Been Tweeked! Is a perfect book for any type of self-improvement discussion group, or to give to all your employees to read!

Group study guide is included in the back of the book.

Available at www.BruceLengeman.com

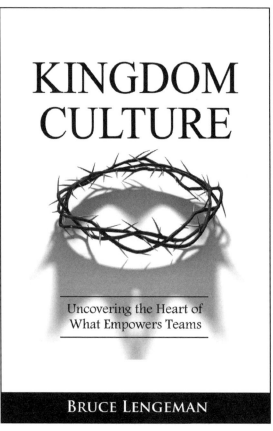

To order more copies of

KINGDOM CULTURE

contact Certa Books

- ❐ Order online at CertaBooks.com/KingdomCulture
- ❐ Call 877-77-CERTA or
- ❐ Email Info@CertaBooks.com

For additional resources from Bruce Lengeman,

visit www.BruceLengeman.com